It's ti

to come home

back 2 God

back 2 His ways

back 2 church

John Jarvis

First published 2005

ISBN: 0-9549509-0-9

Published by
Kingsland Church, Lexden,
2 London Road, Colchester , Essex CO3 4DE

A Charitable Trust Reg. No. 1052819

Designed & Produced by
Footsteps Design & Marketing
alex@footsteps-design.co.uk
www.footsteps-design.co.uk

Acknowledgmants

The development of the back2church website, this book and the associated courses, has been made possible thanks to the inspiration of the Holy Spirit, the encouragement and support of my pastor, Neil Loxley and the practical help of Hayden Andrews, Kevin Ling, Gordon Phillips, Simon Flegg, Nancy Usher and Sally Stephenson. The enthusiasm and technical skills of the Footsteps Design & Marketing team has given us a product beyond our expectations. My thanks to you all.

I am grateful too for my wife Jenny, Joan Smith and others who have supported the project in prayer.

I know the only reward each of you desires is the return of many who used to go to church and that there they will find love and acceptance and will move on to a deeper relationship with our heavenly Father.

It's time... to come home

Contents

This publication is addressed to people who used to attend church services. If you are a 'used to go' person, (there are thousands like you), our prayer is that you will find the contents of this book thought provoking. We want you to know the Church is weakened by your absence and we would love to have you back with us. As a practical expression of our love, we have produced this book and the back2church.org website as a means by which to encourage you to 'think it out again' and come back into fellowship.

The 'we' referred to on this page and elsewhere are a small team from the Kingsland Church Lexden, Colchester, Essex.

The Church is not without blame.

We haven't cared as we should, we have not consistently preached the full gospel, we have not taught believers how to stand firm in the face of temptation and adversity and as one leader has put it; "Some leader's lives have left diminished the example to the flock they should be." Too often we have looked after our own interests instead of "in honour preferring one another" and we have not been open to the leading of the Holy Spirit but have done it our own way. And so we could go on – it's a sorry catalogue of failures. The Kingsland Church congregational leaders, having seen their shortcomings have repented before God and now apologize to you and ask for your forgiveness. We cannot speak for all church fellowships but we know many other church leaders will identify with us in this.

YOU REALLY DO MATTER The Bible is very clear about it. GOD REALLY DOES LOVE YOU! Jesus is the proof of that. The Church belongs to Him and He wants all of us to know Him and His love as part of a church fellowship.

How can a book and a website help?

We believe attending church services or meetings had the potential for something really good in helping to deepen your relationship with God and equipping you for life and service. If that potential had been fully realized, you would belong to a fellowship today. So what happened? In this book we try to help you think back to why you were once part of a church congregation and what caused you to leave. We will look at many of the reasons people leave the fellowship of the Church and suggest some ways by which the many different issues might be resolved. We will then invite you to consider the benefits of getting back into fellowship.

It's true...

Sadly the Church has been its own worst enemy. Its leaders, through compromise with false religion, diluting the truth of the Bible, needless religiosity, a lack of genuine love, disunity and a failure to move with the Holy Spirit, have caused it to lose the clear trumpet call that should be sounding. Paul said: **"If the trumpet does not sound a clear call, who will get ready for battle?"**

(1 Corinthians 14:8)

We accept that over the years, church leaders and their congregations have let many people down in a variety of ways. However, there is hope. There is evidence in many places of the Church waking up – they have 'seen the light' – the need to change and come into line with God's purposes. We believe we are among many church fellowships whose leaders and members have sincerely apologized to God for losing that 'first love' we had for Him, for His word, for one another and for those still to be reached with the good news of the gospel. Please accept our apology for ways in which you feel we have let you down and forgive us. Please, let's start again.

John the Baptist told those who repented and turned towards God's way to **"produce fruit in keeping with repentance." (Matthew 3:8)** The fruit one might expect of the Church's repentance is a change from the many faults we have mentioned above replacing these with a passion for its God-given role which includes:

- a real desire to function as the body of Christ, loving people as He does

- having the same faith in the Scriptures as the Word of God that Jesus demonstrated

- being led by the Holy Spirit as Jesus was

We dare to believe there is a congregation not too far from where you live that has these characteristics.

The production of this book/website is part of our own response when, in the autumn of 2003, the Spirit of God drew to our attention the Church's failure to be what it should be and say what it should say. We hope that through these pages you will find it in your heart to forgive and be reconciled to the Church.

It's time...

Part 1

John Jarvis

Testimonies Helping others Evangelism
eeing people saved/delivered Praise Worship Heali
Prayer ministry Coffee before/after the service
eauty of the building A sense of God's presence The
The warmth of fellowship Sunday school Bible class
me or Cell group The leader The teaching Youth c
l occasions Drama The music group Use of spiritua
g there with the family Having responsibility Taking
Testimonies Helping others Evangelism
eeing people saved/delivered Praise Worship Heali
Prayer ministry Coffee before/after the service
eauty of the building A sense of God's presence The
The warmth of fellowship Sunday school Bible class
me or Cell group The leader The teaching Youth c
l occasions Drama The music group Use of spiritua
g there with the family Having responsibility Taking
Testimonies Helping others Evangelism
eeing people saved/delivered Praise Worship Heali
Prayer ministry Coffee before/after the service
eauty of the building A sense of God's presence The
The warmth of fellowship Sunday school Bible class
me or Cell group The leader The teaching Youth c
l occasions Drama The music group Use of spiritua
g there with the family Having responsibility Taking
Testimonies Helping others Evangelism
eeing people saved/delivered Praise Worship Heali
Prayer ministry Coffee before/after the service
eauty of the building A sense of God's presence The
The warmth of fellowship Sunday school Bible class
me or Cell group The leader The teaching Youth c

Why I Went To Church Meetings

The reason explored

There are probably as many different reasons for starting to attend church as there are fish in the sea. It is still the case that many people are either taken or get sent church, or Sunday school, as a child. I come from a large family – mum and dad had 11 children! Sending us to Sunday school was a way of getting some peace and quiet for a couple of hours one day a week. Some people are invited to go to church by a friend or relative. Others hear about something going on there that sounds interesting and worth a visit. It has been known for some go to find a girl/boy friend! A few will have felt obliged to attend because it was a requirement of a youth organisation they wanted to be part of or the school they attended. Others have turned to the church at a time of great need.

There are many positive reasons why people belong to a church fellowship such as feeling welcome, having good friends who attend, appreciating the style/personality of the pastor/leader/priest, enjoying the services, feeling close to God there, wanting to know more about Christianity or how to live to please God etc. Some speak of it as an opportunity to recharge their spiritual batteries, making them ready to spend another week being light in a world where there is so much darkness.

Take a few moments to think about some of the things you enjoyed about being part of a church congregation. Here are some of the benefits you might have experienced. Put a tick against the ones that were special to you.

The beauty of the building	Use of spiritual gifts
A sense of God's presence	Being there with the family
The music	Having responsibility
The warmth of fellowship	Taking part
Sunday school	Testimonies
Bible class	Helping others
Home or Cell group	Evangelism
The leader	Seeing people saved/delivered
The teaching	Praise
Youth club	Worship
Special occasions	Healing
Drama	Prayer ministry
The music group	Coffee before/after the service

There are probably other benefits we have not mentioned which you can add to this list.

These things that you found helpful are still part of congregational life. If, for whatever reason, those things that were special to you are no longer in the place you used to attend, you will almost certainly find them or something similar in another fellowship of believers not far from where you live. However good these things were, being part of church - the spiritual body of Christ is - more than this. Understanding the true meaning of 'church' helps to give purpose to our attendance and colours our expectations and commitment. We have more to say about this in the section 'The meaning of church'. Getting this right can really make a difference.

Perhaps your experience of what should be beneficial was not good and that is why you left church. Please, don't write off church because of this. I hope to show you that it doesn't have to be this way.

If you did enjoy some of these good things as part of a congregation and no longer go to church, what caused it to come to an end? Perhaps you gradually withdrew as other things crept in that seemed more important than 'church'. Or, was it because your friends thought Christianity irrelevant or laughed at you? Perhaps you felt you couldn't keep up the standards expected of you? Were you disappointed by church in some way? Or, was it something that built up until one day it exploded? Did something go horribly wrong? However you felt, we believe there is a way back. Counsellor and teacher Dr. Neil Anderson, speaking of past hurts says: "We can't fix our pasts, but we can be free from them." The Bible says: **"The truth will set you free." (John 8:32)** To be free to start again will require a truthful look at what happened and a fresh appraisal of the issues in the light of biblical truth. This is what we want to help you to do. The next section 'Reasons I left church' asks 'why?' 'what?' and 'how?' and provides some memory ticklers.

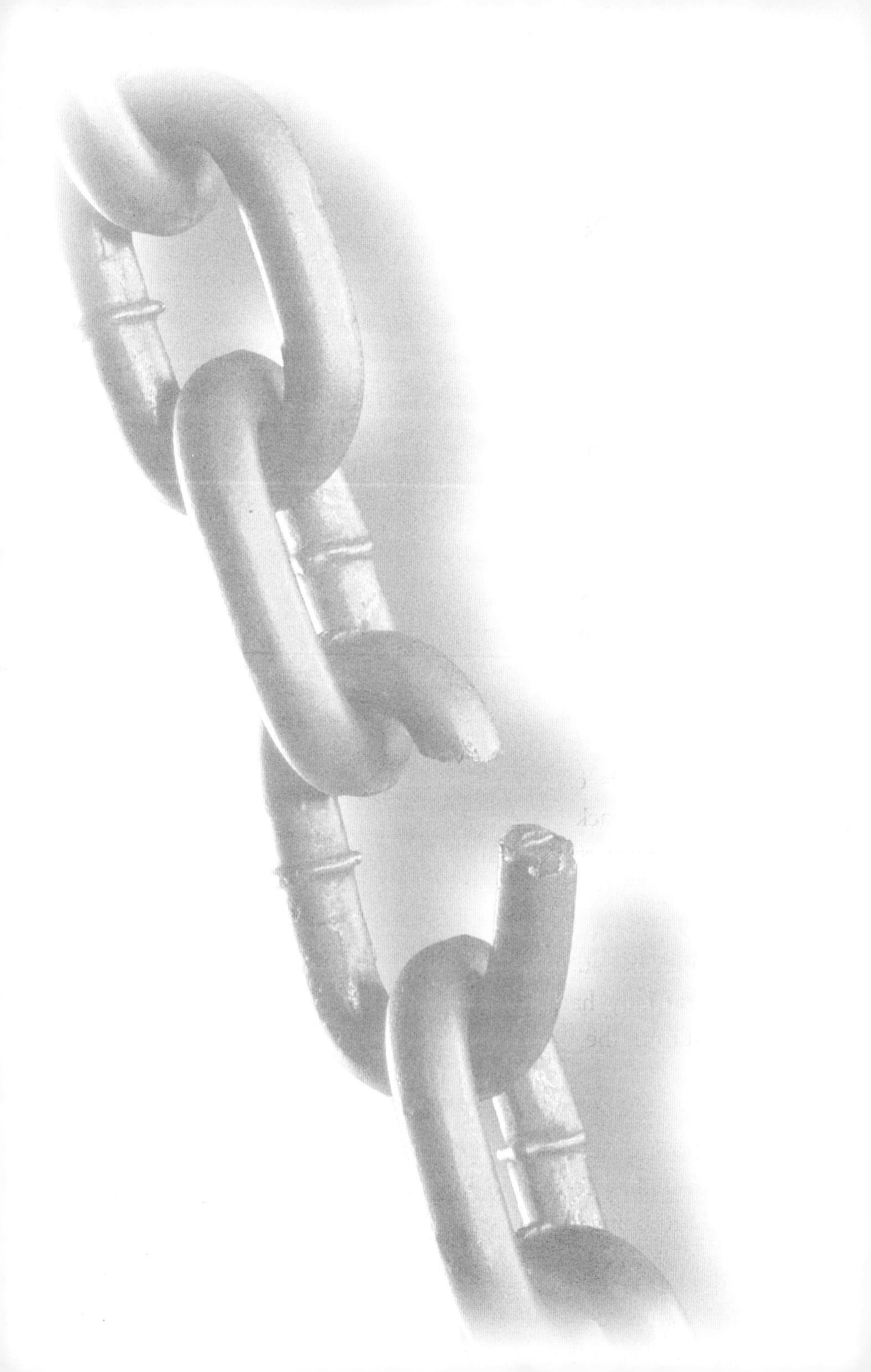

Reason I Left Church

So why did you leave?

Was it boredom, a bit of rebellion, a disagreement, a sin, disillusionment or something else? Was it recently or a long time ago? Whatever the case, we want to offer you help and encouragement to think it through again. There may be serious issues that need to be addressed before you can entertain the idea of getting back into fellowship again. Perhaps these notes will help. You are missed but you are also missing out because the church is changing – there is a new move of God, a new sense of expectancy of a forthcoming time of refreshing and breakthrough. We'd like you to be there with us, enjoying a new relationship with God and in on the action.

We believe Jesus is calling all those who used to attend church services to come back because He loves them and wants them to experience a living relationship with Him and other Christians – enjoying and benefiting from the teaching, worship, discipleship, ministry and mission of the Church in these last days. At a recent meeting, when the subject of those who no longer attend services came up, one lady had a beautiful picture of the hands of Jesus reaching out from the cross to welcome them home. That is how it is with Him!

There is also a sense of urgency that we cannot deny. Prophetic words in the Old and New Testament about the return of Jesus and the end of the age are being fulfilled in our day. Without being alarmist, because those who belong to Christ Jesus have nothing to fear, events of the last 100 years have moved us swiftly to a place where there is a real sense of imminence about the last days. Of course we cannot know when it will be but we can read the signs and they seem to indicate it really won't be long. If you have not made Jesus Lord of your life, we are concerned for you. We don't want you to get left behind when Jesus comes for the church. We want you to be there with us.

Don't let what happened in the past rob you of a glorious future.

Below are some questions you might like to ask yourself to help focus on why you stopped attending church services. May we suggest you write out your answers so you can refer back to them. No one is watching so you can be frank – tell it as it really was.

Questions:

1. When and where did I first attend church services/Sunday school?

2. What was the name of the church fellowship I last attended regularly if different from 1) above?

3. Why did I go to this place of worship?

4. Why did I leave?

5. How did I feel about leaving at the time?

Reasons People Leave The Church

Reasons for leaving

I have put together a list of some of the reasons most frequently given by people for ceasing to attend church services. Then I have grouped them and thought about what I could say that would help you to think it through again. Please read through the reasons below, choose those closest to your response to the questions above and make a note of the reason number(s) for use later.

Group A

1. Found it boring
2. Just decided to leave
3. Friends or relatives left, so I did
4. I got nothing out of going – it did nothing for me
5. Moved away and then didn't bother
6. Other things gradually took up my time
7. There were no potential girl/boyfriends there

Group B

8. Didn't feel welcome
9. Didn't see much evidence of love there
10. I thought they were snobbish
11. I felt I wasn't good enough

Group C

12. I had to leave – misbehaved
13. I couldn't keep up the standard

and felt a failure - hypocrite

14. Got into things that are not Christian
15. I was single and pregnant and felt embarrassed/judged
16. I had an abortion and knew they wouldn't like that
17. I was sent to prison

Group D

18. Didn't agree with some of the things they believed or preached
19. Didn't agree with some of the things that were done
20. Felt they were hypocrites and wanted nothing more to do with them

Group E

21. They were always on about money
22. Wanted me to give them more of my income – couldn't afford it
23. The church misused our money or assets

Group F

24. I was so involved, it took up too much time – caused family upset

Group G

25. Was hurt, misunderstood, felt rejected or passed over
26. Thought no one really listened to my point of view
27. Where were they when I needed them?
28. I am disappointed with God
29. I am not sure I believe in God anymore

Group H

30. My spouse/partner doesn't want me to attend church
31. I could attend but don't want to go without my spouse/partner, who won't

Group I

32. I got divorced and was made to feel guilty
33. I got divorced and remarried.
    Felt the Church couldn't cope with that

Group J

34. I can't find a church fellowship I like

Group K

35. I can't get to a church building of my choice without help with transport

Action

To get to the comments on your particular reason(s) more quickly, you could now skip to the section below incorporating that reason. If you do this, I recommend you come back to the 'review' at some time and look at all the comments because they contain some important principles that are worth knowing anyway.

of the things
believed or preached

I couldn't kee
up the standar
and felt a failur
- hypocrite

nted me to give them more of
y income - couldn't afford it

I WAS SINGLE AND
PREGNANT AND FELT
ARRASSED/JUDGED

I am not sure I believe in God anym

t into things that are not Christi

I had to leave – misbehave

got divorced and remarri

I got divorced and was made to feel gu

Didn't agree with
ome of the things
that were done

Where w
they wh
I needed

ad an abortion and knew
they wouldn't like that

MY SPOUSE PARTN
DOESN T WANT M
TO ATTEND CHURC

am disappointed with G

The Reasons Reviewed

(Group A. Incorporating reasons 1-7)

An Affair Of The Heart

Boring! It did nothing for me. I saw no reason to stay

If you were bored in church services, I apologize. Services should never be boring but they can be when they seem irrelevant to our daily lives, lack conviction, or when the life of the Holy Spirit is not in evidence and love is not felt. However, they may also be boring if our purpose in being at a service is other than that for which church services are intended. When a congregation meets it should be for worship, for prayer, for drawing closer to God, for hearing His Word use of spiritual gifts and a time for fellowship and encouraging one another. What do we mean by these terms and what difference do they make as to whether or not a service is boring or irrelevant?

Worship

To worship God is to fulfil what Jesus called **"The greatest commandment"** which is **"Love the Lord your God with all your heart and with all your soul and with all your mind and with all your strength." (Mark 12:30)**. True Christians are those who know that God loves them – they have seen his love in Jesus and the cross – and their response is to love Him with all their heart. Jesus also **said, "True worshippers will worship the Father in spirit and in truth." (John 4:23)**. As Rick Warren has said "Worship is our spirit responding to God's Spirit."

In many churches the term 'Worship' is used to replace what once was called 'singing a hymn or chorus' but as we have said, worship is much more than singing. It is a life-style of commitment to a relationship with our loving heavenly Father. However, it is a fact that God delights in hearing His people express their worship of Him through music and song. Sadly, many church congregations know how to sing but don't know how to worship in song. Is there a difference? There certainly is! When we truly worship, the focus of our music, singing and praying will not be on us – on our ability to perform or on our needs - but on God. The more we concentrate on Him, the more likely it is that His Spirit will make His presence felt – and then anything can happen! An increasing number of congregations are experiencing the weighty presence of God as the worship of their hearts finds expression in music and song. In this manifest Presence they often find an overwhelming sense of God's love, healings may take place, some people are convicted of their need of Jesus, others receive direction for their lives or revelation of a special work God wants them to do and troubled minds find a peace that passes understanding or a new perspective on life. Boring? I don't think so!

Prayer

A prayer is a request. Jesus encourages us to make prayers to Father God in His name and tells us to **"Ask and it will be given to you; seek and you will find; knock and the door will be opened to you." (Luke 11:9)**. But He also tells us we must ask in faith believing the Father loves to answer prayer. When we pray according to His known will and in agreement with one another, we can expect answers to our prayers. Often it's a "Yes," sometimes a "Yes but not yet, keep on believing," and occasionally a "No, I have a better plan." The delays and silences of God are always ultimately for our good – never because He does not love us.

Praying together as a congregation is an expression of unity in asking that God's **"will be done on earth as it is in heaven." (Matthew 6:10)**. What the world needs most at this time is Jesus, the light of the world to dispel the darkness of evil. When we pray together it does make a difference. God is at work in these days by His Spirit in nations, cities and town like never before - in answer to the prayers of His people.

Praying for one another is part of serving. When we pray relying on the Holy Spirit to guide us it's powerful! It is part of the life of the Church.

Drawing closer to God

We draw closer to God as we truly worship and pray. God not only wants us to speak to Him but He wants to communicate with us too. He most often speaks to us through His Word, the Bible but also through spiritual gifts and direct to our hearts. The more we focus on Him, the more likely we are to hear His still, small voice speaking to us. It is through communication that relationships develop. It is the same in our relationship with God.

Communion, or the Lord's Supper, can be a very special time because it is not only a reminder of the Cross but also of Christ's victory that we take into our body as we eat the bread. And as we drink from the cup we enjoy the wonder of the New Covenant in His blood whereby we have access to God through Jesus.

The promise we have is, **"Come near to God and He will come near to you." (James 4:8)**. Come near to Love and Love will come near to you. What more could we want?

Hearing His Word

A leader who believes the Scriptures are inspired by God, makes them the basis of his/her own life and listens to the Holy Spirit, will be able to inspire their congregation to have confidence in the Bible as God's Word. Then there will be an expectancy to hear from God through his preaching and teaching. Such leaders can help their congregations to 'walk in the Spirit' - be led by Him and enjoy victory over the things they would otherwise struggle with. When leaders water down the Bible message, people don't know where they stand and confusion reigns. In these days of the increasing activity of the enemy of our souls, leaders must be able to show their congregation the relevance of the Bible to everyday life. The Bible warns leaders who are not faithful in this ministry that they will be severely judged by our Lord. (This is such a serious matter but unless we also spend time reading the Bible, how will we know if we are being led astray?) God has chosen preaching and teaching as one of the ways He talks to us. If we are not listening, what are we missing?

Use of spiritual gifts

God has poured out His Spirit just as He promised and the Holy Spirit imparts to those who are willing to receive, spiritual gifts for the common good. Paul tells us to **"eagerly desire spiritual gifts"** and **"try to excel in gifts that build up the church." (1 Corinthians 14:1&12)**. Clearly without these gifts which Paul describes in his first letter to the Corinthian church, there is something missing that is of importance to the well being of the church. The gifts He wants you to excel in will be a blessing to the Church but not if you are not there! If you have not received teaching on the value of spiritual gifts, you will find information on how to obtain this under the heading of 'Resources' at the end of the book.

A time for fellowship and encouragement

When a congregation meets together, unless there is time before or after the service to talk to one another – preferable over a cup of tea or coffee, there is no real fellowship. In my own congregation, I sometimes think as much 'ministry' is done at this time as can result from an altar call. It happens as we express our love for one another and interest in each other's joys, sorrows, experiences of life and in sharing our faith. It is an opportunity to get to know new comers and visitors. It is part of building one another up in the faith.
Wouldn't you like to be part of this in a church near you?

A love that is attractive

Coming together for the reasons above can result in unity of spirit and caring for one another in love that is attractive. In such an atmosphere it is easier to invite others – especially those who are not believers - to come along. Also when church services are like this, people find encouragement to grow in their relationship with God and with others who want this too and they will want to discover how they can use what God has made them to be for His service. They will want to avail themselves of everything God offers by way of spiritual gifts so as to use them for the glory of God.

Sounds ideal? But there isn't a perfect church because it is made up of people and we blow it sometimes. However, maybe you are thinking "If I had the opportunity of a church like this, perhaps I wouldn't have left." It is not too late to start again.

If nothing has changed

What should you do if you want to experience the kind of church we have described above but have been put off returning to your former church because you know for a fact that the services are not like this but are still just boring? (Could this be why so many church buildings have closed down?). You have a choice – to go there and work for change or go elsewhere. If you think you should stay and work for change, it is vital that you walk in the light with the leader. You must tell him/her the truth about how you feel and that if you return, you will be asking God to change things, otherwise he or she may be unaware there is a problem. A leader may be challenged by this and want to take a serious look at his/her ministry. Some however, will prefer to take their cue from those who like things the way they are. Others may be afraid to make changes that will go against someone in the church with strong opinions or financial leverage. However, I know of instances where Christians have prayed, asking God to break into their leader's life with fresh revelation in order to change their ministry for the good - or remove him. It worked!

It is a fact that in a congregation, a change for the good at 'grass roots' level seldom works without change of heart in the leadership. A decision to stay in a 'dry' situation and work for change should be time limited. If at the end of this time there has been no real improvement, you should seek God again about the matter. It may be that you need to start looking for another church fellowship. To stop attending church altogether is not the answer

We are meant to enjoy the positive input of church fellowship and teaching and without it our Christianity will be hard pressed to withstand the pressure of the world to conform to its ways. Compromise stands at the door and knocks! Few can hold out alone indefinitely. It is better to make a fresh start elsewhere than grow cold in our faith.

A heart issue

It is possible to be part of a congregation where the worship is (according to everyone else) wonderful, the Holy Spirit is at work as witnessed by prophecies, words of wisdom and knowledge, healings and anointed teaching and yet still be bored. When our heart does not really want to be part of church life, our mind takes the cue and wanders all over the place - especially down the road of criticism! Many other reasons given for leaving the fellowship of the church find their root here.

Earlier in the section 'The reason I left church' you were asked why you went to church. What was your answer? Only if you can say it is because you know it is God's chosen way of helping us develop our relationship with Him and with one another are you on the right track.

A coach and wild horses

Being part of a congregation for the right reason makes all the difference in the world. If we go for all the right reasons, it will take a coach and wild horses to stop us going. It will be immaterial whether or not our friends or relatives stop attending. Not only will we be fully committed, we will try to win them back!

The value of fellowship

In many parts of the world today, Christians face persecution and are forced to meet secretly because church services have been outlawed by those in power. Such Christians value the benefits of meeting together so highly that nothing but imprisonment or serious injury can keep them away. The desire for fellowship is so strong that Christians in prison for their faith frequently risk further punishment by telling other prisoners the good news about God's love. If those they tell become disciples, there is then the encouragement and personal strengthening gained as a result of fellowship with these new believers. Many a church has been started in prison.

God wants a relationship with us

In extreme circumstances it is possible to have a rewarding relationship with God without attending church services. This letter from a listener to Feba Radio Christian Broadcasts in Ethiopia is a case in point:-

"I live in a remote area where there are no churches or any kind of Christian presence. In fact if you're found to be a Christian the local people look at you as a weird person. I feel that your radio ministry is a God sent messenger that regularly comes to me to rescue me from destruction. I really thank God for your ministry."

For this believer, Feba Radio is the church because there is nothing else. We thank God for ministries such as Feba Radio, United Christian Broadcasters, the God Channel and others who help fill this gap. But most people in the west are not deprived in this way. Christianity is all about relationships: about God loving us; us loving God, loving others and being loved by them. The fellowship of the Church is God's chosen way of helping us to build up our relationship with Him and other Christians – the Church is His.

All manner of places

The New Testament Church met in all manner of places – there were no church buildings then but they turned the world upside down (Acts 17:6) by their response to the love of God. In loving Him and desiring to put Him first in everything and be led by the Holy Spirit, they walked in love for one another and changed the world. This is because their heart was in it! God can do this for each one of us.

The highest priority

Putting our heart right with God should be a higher priority than finding the right place of worship. When we are right with God and ask Him to show us the congregation we should be part of, He will lead us there. If our heart is right, we will have an inner peace that this detail will be taken care of. How do we get right with Him? By putting Him first! This means admitting we haven't always made Him and His will our priority. It is also helpful to confess this to a fellow Christian too - one we respect so they can pray for us – **"Therefore confess your sins to each other and pray for each other... (James 5:16)**. It means asking for and receiving His forgiveness and inviting the Holy Spirit to come and fill us with Himself.

Beginning a relationship with God

If you have never invited Jesus into your life, you can do so by speaking out the 'Prayer to become a Christian'. You will find this under the section 'Suggestions for prayer'. Having prayed this prayer, make daily fellowship with God by reading the Bible and prayer your first priority. Then either go back to the fellowship you left or find somewhere else that you can commit to. For help with the latter see the section 'Getting back or moving on'.

We give a fuller explanation of the purpose of the church in the section 'The meaning of Church'.

(Group B. Incorporating reasons 8 -11)

Being In The Right Place

The title is a play on words. It is about being in the right church fellowship but more importantly, about being in a right place with God. We have to admit, with shame, that some congregations act like exclusive clubs and it can be very hard for a newcomer to get 'in'. This is not how 'church' is meant to be. In such a situation we can either stay and work for change or leave and go where we feel welcome and accepted. Feeling 'at home' in a congregation is important but being in a right place with God is even more so.

A spiritual right place

We are in a right place with God when we know our sins are forgiven, have the inner witness of the Holy Spirit that God really does love us and we show our love for Him by being obedient to His Word and the prompting of the Holy Spirit. This in turn leads us to love and forgive others and a sense of peace in our own spirit.

Only when we are in this right place can we properly handle any negative attitudes coming from other members of the congregation. Where there is little evidence of love or people are made to feel unwelcome or not good enough, we should take our concerns to the leader. He /she will be more likely to listen to us if our lives don't exhibit the very attitudes we are complaining about. We should not simply dump the problem on the leader however but seek to work with him or her to bring about change as well as praying fervently for this to happen.

The church as a right place

If we are in a right place with God but the leader of the congregation doesn't want to know what is going on or feels there is nothing he/she can do about people being made to feel unwelcome or not good enough, we should ask God if we are in the right congregation. If we ask and expect to get an answer, He promises we will! **"If you believe, you will receive whatever you ask for in prayer." (Matthew 21:22)** However, we must always be prepared for God to say "Yes, in spite of the difficulties, I want you here." He knows what's around the corner – He may have something up His sleeve that is going to turn things around in which you could play a key role. Friends of ours were in a fellowship that seemed to be going downhill fast and the warnings given to the leadership seemed to fall on deaf ears. They began to ask God "Are You sure You want us here?" and were sorely tempted to leave. Encouraged through a prophetic word to stick it out and keep on praying blessings on the fellowship resulted not only in a change of leadership but they found themselves part of it!

On the other hand, the answer to your prayer might equally be a sense of peace that going elsewhere is what God wants you to do. Although a sense of peace is an important indicator anyway, He may also confirm you should move in other ways such as dreams, invitations from friends, an advertisement or a verse of Scripture. A decision to leave should be explained to the leader of the church fellowship and you should bend over backwards to leave with a good grace.

Getting our heart in the right place

What if the real reason behind our criticism of the congregation is that our heart is not in the right place with God? There really is only one remedy and that is to humble ourselves, agree with God that He is right and we are wrong, ask His forgiveness then turn around and go His way. As we invite the Holy Spirit to take control of that area of our lives, we will find peace and the strength to change. If you are not used to praying in this way, you will find a Prayer of Repentance in the section 'Suggestions for prayer'. Having made this prayer, your relationship with God will be restored. Now get back into fellowship, apologize and enjoy being part of a congregation once again.

(Group C. Incorporating reasons 12 - 17)

When Worlds Collide

The Christian gospel is such good news because God gives those who trust Him all the strength they need to be victorious over the flesh, the world and the devil. And when we fail, He doesn't write us off but gives us the opportunity to renounce the wrong we have done, to change our minds, seek His forgiveness and go His way. He promises to forgive us when we ask and then helps us overcome next time we are tempted, so long as we set our hearts on pleasing Him.

The battleground

We know the spiritual and natural worlds are on a collision course – one of them has to go. Paul says to the Galatians: **"So I say, live by the Spirit, and you will not want to gratify the desires of the sinful nature. For the sinful nature desires what is contrary to the Spirit, and the Spirit what is contrary to the sinful nature. They are in conflict with each other." (Galatians 5:16/17)**. The Greek word he uses for 'sinful nature' can also be translated as 'flesh.' Our nature (flesh) is sinful and remains so until we are set free through our confession of faith in the blood of Jesus to wash us clean.

We must choose

Whilst receiving God's forgiveness for past sins is a vital part of becoming a Christian, making Jesus Lord of our lives and choosing to live by the Spirit is just as important. Paul tells us that **"Those who belong to Christ Jesus have crucified the sinful nature (flesh) with its passions and desires." (Galatians 5:24)**. Trying to please God whilst retaining the ways of our old sinful nature doesn't work! While we do this we will always feel guilty in God's presence and when we are among His true followers. The bottom line is we have to choose between God and our sinful nature. If we choose God, then every time we are tempted to go back to our old ways, or do something we know God doesn't want us to do, He will give us a way out of the temptation – God promises **"No temptation has seized you except what is common to man. And God is faithful; he will not let you be tempted beyond what you can bear. But when you are tempted, He will also provide a way out so that you can stand up under it." (1 Corinthians 10:13)**.

Walking by the Spirit

What did the apostle Paul mean when he told the early believers to 'walk by the Spirit'? In the simplest terms, once we have made Jesus our Saviour and Lord, He calls us to open up every area of our lives to the Holy Spirit. As He shows us any sins or attachments we have that are out of character with His holiness, He wants us to choose to confess, receive forgiveness through the blood of Jesus and decide to give up those things that are not of Him and instead go His way. We then ask Him to fill with Himself all the areas of our life that are now clean. Made clean and filled with His joy and power we move from being under circumstances to being on top. The more readily we respond to His promptings, the more we will sense His presence and direction on our path.

If you have never received any teaching on the Holy Spirit, I strongly recommend attending an Alpha Course that includes teaching on this matter. Alternatively, there are also some good books and teaching tapes available on the subject. Details are to be found under the section 'Resources'.

Saints sometimes sin

The apostle John tells us **"No-one who lives in Him keeps on sinning"** but we do sometimes sin. When we fail, God is so good to us that if we confess our sin, determine to give it up, ask for His forgiveness and turn away from our sin, He will forgive and clean us up. **"If we confess our sins, He is faithful and just and will forgive us our sins and purify us from all unrighteousness." (1 John 1:9)**. What a wonderful Saviour! If only we were as generous with our forgiveness as God is!

There is power in confession

When we blow it we may assume the church fellowship will be critical and unforgiving but if we confess our sin and make appropriate restitution, we will almost certainly find forgiveness and encouragement to put the past behind us and start again. The Bible tells us to **"...confess your sins to each other and pray for each other so that you may be healed." (James 5:16)**. If a congregation is unwilling to forgive we should consider going to a different Christian place of worship but in this case, we should a) tell the leader of the fellowship that we are leaving why and b) inform the leader of the new congregation about our past sin, our efforts to put things right with the leader and congregation and why we decided to leave.

Action

God loves you and wants to forgive. Pray the Prayer of Repentance in 'Suggestions for Prayer'. When we do our part and confess our sins, we can be sure He will do his part and forgive and purify us. Then you can either return to your former congregation or if this is not practical, inform the leader of your decision to make a new start before finding a new place. Be honest with the leader of the congregation you hope to join about why you left and of your repentance. Seek his/her help as you start living to please God and enjoying fellowship with Him and His people. Ask for help in learning who you are in Christ Jesus and how to overcome in areas where you have failed or are vulnerable.

Perhaps I have committed the unforgivable sin

It is surprising how many people worry if they have committed the 'unforgivable sin.' It is unlikely that anyone who has will ever choose to turn to Christ Jesus for forgiveness, whereas you have, so put this thought out of your mind. It is an old trick of the devil – the father of lies - to try and deceive us in this matter.

Pregnancy outside of marriage

The Church has genuine concerns about this and in each case has to do a balancing act between compassion and maintaining its position that the right time to have children is within a loving married relationship. It is a fact that the Church has not always shown compassion to unmarried mothers and has too many times turned its back on them. Though fathers involved are sometimes made to suffer as well, it seems the women generally bear the brunt of the condemnation. Although there are still some places like that, thank God that the truth about His amazing grace is replacing the cold, legalistic views that so many church leaders once held. Today there is much greater willingness to face the reality that pregnancies outside of marriage do happen and leaders are more inclined to be supportive.

This does not mean the Church has changed its mind – it still sees fathering a child and pregnancy outside of marriage as wrong but it is not unforgivable. Where there is recognition that this is not God's way and a real intention to give up these ways and turn towards God, forgiveness can be sought and will be given. To be accepted into fellowship, the parent(s) must be willing to work with the leader of that fellowship in turning the situation around for good. This way of looking at pregnancy outside of marriage can be difficult for a congregation to cope with if they have been taught the legalistic view. There will be some who think if the Church doesn't show its disapproval one of the fundamental reasons for marriage will be lost. However, when the Church asks "What would Jesus do?" it always finds forgiveness and love.

Church leaders are well aware of the fact that pregnancies are sometimes the result of a woman being abused. When this happens, what is required is healing and compassion not condemnation. It would be an exceptionally hard hearted leader who would refuse this.

True repentance opens doors

If you have stopped being part of a congregation because you are the mother or father of a child born or, to be born outside of marriage, talk to your church leader. We will be surprised if he/she doesn't want to discuss a way forward that will have inclusion rather than exclusion as its aim. Be prepared to acknowledge if the pregnancy has not come about in circumstances that are in line with the model God has given to us in his Word and that He is right and you were wrong to have let this happen. However, God is love – He can't help it and He forgives those who truly repent and will be with them to help them and the child through all the difficulties these situations can bring.

When a pregnancy is the result of rape and the mother bravely chooses to go ahead with the pregnancy, the support of a loving church fellowship will be of tremendous value. Overcoming anger and false shame may be major hurdles for the mother but the Church can point her to One who unconditionally accepts her and help her find the freedom that comes from being able to forgive.

Further help in matters of divorce and abortion

Because failed marriages and abortions are issues that affect a lot of people and can leave deep scars, we have included on the website courses that can be of real help to those in this situation. Meanwhile, be assured that although divorce and/or abortion are serious matters, neither is unforgivable.

(Group D. Incorporating reasons 18 - 20)

Leaders Can Be Wrong!

It would be surprising if church members never disagreed with their leader or among themselves. It would not be real and God is not shocked when it happens. Church leaders are generally sincere in their commitment to pastor their flock but they can sometimes be sincerely wrong. However, so can we! This is one of the reasons the Bible tells us so many times to know, love and meditate on the Word. The Bible tells us what to do when these problems arise. That is why if you have a disagreement about what your leader teaches, you should make time to sit down with him / her and go through what the Bible has to say on the subject or the biblical principles involved. Ask the Holy Spirit "Please lead us to the truth on this matter. I surrender my opinions and will let God's Word be the final arbiter." In this attitude, most problems can easily be resolved. If you and your leader then still think your different stand points can both be justified in Scripture, find another leader who you both respect and ask for their help.

These same principles can be applied in dealing with things the leader approves of but you don't. Everything must be done in love - not to pull down or destroy. Many times if we made the effort to check things out with the Scriptures and discuss the issue with our leader in an attitude of humility, agreement would be reached and leaving the fellowship would be out of the question. Remember, when checking out what the Bible says it is vital to consider the context in which the verses were written; to whom were they addressed – the Jews, the nations or the Church and how are they to be interpreted in the light of other Scriptures?

If you left a church without trying to resolve differences, it will rob you of your peace. Do something about it!

If a congregation or its leader does not practise what it preaches, you could cry "Hypocrisy!" and leave. But will running away from the problem really help to put it right? Confront the issue with the leader, first making very sure your own attitude is one of love and genuine concern. Pray that the eyes of those involved will be opened to the truth of the Word of God and to the hypocrisy of their position. If you can see it and it is true, the likelihood is others in the congregation will also see it and will be praying about it. Expect God to answer your prayers and bring the situation to a head so it can be dealt with. Only if a leader stubbornly refuses to repent of a wrong doing should you think about leaving – even then, check it out with God – let the peace of God rule your heart in the matter.

Be aware that our adversary the devil is always looking to give you some reason to leave the fellowship of a church. If he is allowed to have his way, he will take a small thing and build it up into something big. Stop him in his tracks. **"Resist the devil, and he will flee from you. Come near to God and He will come near to you. (James 4:7/8)**.

If, on reflection, you have fallen for one of his tricks, ask for God's forgiveness, apologize to the leader and get back on track with Him – get back to church.

(Group E. Incorporating reasons 21 - 23)

Money, Money, Money

Money matters

1. The Church needs money to function

2. Church buildings have to be maintained. If the congregation does not have a building of its own but hires somewhere for its services, the hire charge must be paid.

3. If a fellowship wants the benefits of a paid leader or team of leaders, Scripture says they should be given double honour i.e. paid a decent salary. (I Timothy 5:17).

4. The cost of administration must be met. Secretarial services, telephone, stationary, advertising etc. are basic to the running of a fellowship.

5. The programme put on for and by the congregation i.e. discipleship training, worship, evangelism and other outreach requires money for music, sound systems, literature etc.

6. Visiting speakers should be rewarded for their labour and their costs met.

7. The congregation should follow the model of the early church in also giving outside to support missions and other Christian works

8. What about the relief of poverty?
... And so we could go on.

In an ideal world, every congregation would be self supporting and able to sow into other developing churches and missions. Where is this money to come from? US! No, not the USA, but you and me.

Most people who go to church services are happy to give to the church funds. Some will also give to 'missions' such as Christian aid, Tear fund, Open Doors, medical missions etc. However, what most people don't like is being told what to give. The model of tithing that is being urged on believers across the denominations a lot these days is not always well received. It may be argued that tithing is an Old Covenant thing since the only reference to it in the New Testament which proponents use is where the writer of Hebrews takes an Old Testament story that mentions tithing to make a point. However, the point he is making (Hebrews chapter seven), is not about giving but the priesthood of Christ Jesus. It is a fact that neither Jesus nor the apostles commanded anything concerning tithes or how much believers should give. However, Jesus and the apostles spoke about and encouraged giving.

It is a sad fact that some leaders have put their faith in the tithing system for their personal support instead of in God. Some have used tithing as a rod with which to beat their flock and caused considerable resentment in the process.

Giving is a heart issue

Giving is a heart issue. The more we understand and appreciate what

God has done for us in Christ Jesus, the more we want to express our thanks. I almost wrote 'express our thanksgiving'. Interesting isn't it that we combine these words 'thanks' and 'giving'. Someone has said "Love's prerogative is to give and give." Jesus applauded the widow who gave all she had into the Temple funds and the apostle Paul commended the believers in Macedonia saying: **"Out of the most severe trial, their overflowing joy and their extreme poverty welled up in rich generosity. For I testify that they gave as much as they were able, and even beyond their ability." (2 Corinthians 8:2/3)**. Their giving was sacrificial - a practical expression of their love.

The Malachi 3:8-12 passage which strong advocates of tithing quote, contains a spiritual principle we can't ignore whatever we feel about tithing. God says in effect, **"If you will, then I will." "Bring the whole tithe into the storehouse that there may be food in My house. Test me in this," says the Lord Almighty, "and see if I will not throw open the floodgates of heaven and pour out so much blessing that you will not have room enough for it."**

Our Lord Jesus said a similar thing, **"Give, and it will be given to you. A good measure, pressed down, shaken together and running over will be poured into your lap. For with the measure you use, it will be measured to you." (Luke 6:38)**.

How much should we give?

So how much should we give? Paul gives some sound advice in his letter to the Corinthians 9:6-8. **"Remember this: Whoever sows sparingly will also reap sparingly, and whoever sows generously, will also reap generously. Each man should give what he has**

decided in his heart to give, not reluctantly or under compulsion, for God loves a cheerful giver. And God is able to make all grace abound to you, so that in all things at all times, having all that you need, you will abound in every good work."

For many people, to move from putting change in the offering to give a tenth of their income to the Church is quite a step of faith but it is this faith which pleases God – He wants us to trust Him for our provision. If sowing a tenth of your income into the Church does not require faith because you have more than enough to be able to do this, consider whether you should be doing more. The important thing is to seek God about what to give and obey Him – cheerfully.

Many Christians believe giving a tenth of their income is a good place to start. It is a fact that when some people start to give in this way they get blessed almost overnight. Others give their tenth for years but never experience Malachi's 'opening of the floodgates of heaven to pour out so much blessing that you don't have room for it all.' Why? It could be that those who are instantly blessed are being encouraged by God because their heart is right. It may be that for others the delay (it can only be a delay because God is faithful – His Word is true) is because He first wants to do a work in their hearts. This work might be to produce faith that will persevere - James 1:2-4 shows us how important this is. God may be working on an attitude which might be grudging when it should be joyful - remember God loves a cheerful giver. It could be that He wants them first to seek the kingdom of God and his righteousness – Matthew 6:33 - or to teach them the secret of being content whatever the circumstances – Philippians 4:10-13.

Giving cheerfully

If you left church over the giving of money matter, make sure your heart is right. If you are giving in line with the Word of God – generously, cheerfully and in faith, it really should not be an issue as you to learn to trust Him in this key area of your commitment to Him.

If you think you can't afford to give, go before God, get your heart right and ask for His help. To some He gives faith to tithe and trust Him to make ends meet. Others make a decision that being a generous giver is where they really want to be, so they make a start by giving sacrificially. They then determine that out of the increase God provides, they will give more than a tenth of this increase and continue to act in this way until they are where they want to be in their overall giving.

Don't be robbed

Don't let Satan rob you of the fellowship, teaching, service, worship and joy of being part of His Body – the Church - over this matter. Trust God – His promises are "yes" and "amen" in Christ Jesus. (2 Corinthians 1:20) Talk to the leader, tell them about your concerns and agree in prayer that God will stir up your faith, show you what to give and prosper you as you obey, in His time.

The church as steward

If you left a congregation because you didn't agree with how money was being used, did you first go through all the right channels to express your views? Did you really listen to the reasons for using the money in that particular way? Did you talk to the Lord about it and ask Him to show you or the leader(s) if you or they were wrong. As we have said, leaders can get it wrong sometimes but so can we. If you were still convinced you were right but the leader was not persuaded, did others in the congregation also feel uncomfortable about the leader's position in the matter? If so, did you together take it to the church leaders? It would be most unusual for church leaders to ignore such an approach, however, as we have said, leaders do sometimes get it wrong.

Was it really such a big issue that the years of fellowship and working together for the Kingdom you enjoyed were left in tatters? Was this the real issue or were you looking for an excuse to leave anyway? Was there a matter of pride you needed to deal with? It's not too late to get back to God on the matter and to apologize. It's time to get back to church! It's time to forgive and forget! It's time for a new beginning! It's later than you think!

(Group F. Incorporating reason 24)

Confused Priorities

No one is surplus

In a larger congregation we may be tempted to think, "Relax and enjoy it, there are plenty willing to take responsibility, I don't need to get involved." The truth is there is no one surplus to requirements in the Church. God has a plan for all who put their trust in Him and if we seek Him, He will reveal it to us and create opportunity for it to happen.

Spinning plates

In smaller congregations, the devil often uses the opposite trick. Whenever there is a vacant position he will look for someone on whom he can lay guilt about the task not being done. Often he will choose someone who is already up to their neck trying to keep things running. Another trick is to make us feel we have to keep going even when our circumstances change and we have insufficient time for all that needs to be done. Sadly the one who tries to keep all these plates spinning then collapses with exhaustion, feeling guilty and Satan laughs!

People v. programmes

God wants us to serve one another. He wants willing people whose desire is to see the Church grow and play a useful part in the community. A church programme can help facilitate these things but God is more interested in us as individuals than any programme. Reflecting His glory in our relationships at home, work and leisure as well as church is what gets His attention. Because of this He wants leaders who will protect their flock from over-busyness and spiritual-burn out that can lead to neglecting family and friends and squeeze out our daily time with God, reading the Bible and prayer.

Filling the gaps

As is the case with leaders in business, church leaders are taught one of the secrets of success in leadership is to delegate – to free themselves of trying to do everything and use the variety of gifts in their congregation. This is good because it enables people to develop and grow and find satisfaction in serving. There is often a gap however between what needs to be done and the people available to do it, especially in smaller congregations. What is then required of the leadership is a willingness to discuss priorities openly with their congregation letting them feel they can say 'No' without guilt being laid on them. This can be hard if some aspect of church life has to cease because of the new reality. To leave a congregation because of too much involvement should never happen because then everyone loses out. If this really was your reason for leaving, please think again and talk to the leader – there must be a way through that will keep things in balance.

Facing the truth

It has to be said that leaving church for the above reason only is rare. More often than not, it is the straw that broke the camels back type of situation. In reality there were other issues and over busyness provided the excuse needed to bring to an end something you were not happy with anyway? If there were other issues, perhaps it's time to find out the real cause. Go back to the list of reasons for leaving church and see if you can identify those that are nearest to your underlying reason. Check out what this guide says about the true reason. The truth will set you free!

(Group G. Incorporating reasons 25 - 27)

Does Anybody Care?

God cares

Yes, God cares, more than you may think. He has shown us how very much He cares in Jesus and the cross. Jesus paid the price of caring with His own life blood. He has called us in love to come to Him, cast our cares on Him and trust Him to take care of us. He has given us the Holy Spirit to comfort and guide us. He has given us the Church in which to develop loving relationships, find fulfilment in serving one another and be equipped to tell others of the good news of His love. God really does care!

Who else cares?

Leaders in the Church care because they have a responsibility not only to proclaim the good news of the gospel but also to make of converts disciples who know who they are in Christ Jesus, trust Him and walk in obedience – loving Him and one another. Most leaders recognize they are under-shepherds who have to give an account of their ministry to the Chief Shepherd. There is always the exception to the rule but most church leaders take the care of their flock seriously – it's not just their job - the love of Christ constrains them to. A leader who doesn't care is in big trouble because he/she will be judged twice as hard as the rest of us. Such a leader doesn't deserve your company – find another church!

Who will meet my needs?

There is much misunderstanding about what it means for a church and its leaders to care. Preacher Rick Joiner has quite rightly said, "Church is not there to meet people's needs but to point them to the One who can." Often we get hurt because we look to people to meet our need instead of to Jesus. He knows we need to feel we are accepted, secure and significant and He is able to meet all of these needs all the time whereas people can only partially meet our needs for just some of the time. As we seek God's help in the name of Jesus with the support of the leader or whoever he/she appoints, God will use them to speak into our lives His counsel.

Home groups

Many churches have discovered the benefits of developing home groups (also known as cell groups, discipleship groups etc). Home group leaders care because one of the purposes of these groups is usually the pastoral care of the members as well as encouragement in their mission. Because the groups are generally small in number there is opportunity to really get to know one another, pray for each other and help in practical ways with needs as they arise.

Becoming mature

God wants us all to develop into mature believers using the gifts we have to serve one another and build up the church. He does not want us to remain as spiritual babies. He wants us to grow up! We all start as spiritual babies. To grow up we must feed on the Word in our own devotional times and by listening to sermons and teaching tapes. Just as we grow in our relationships with people by spending time with them, so it is with God. As this relationship with Him develops we start to rely less on feelings and more on who He is and His love for us. As we take time to fellowship with other believers we find **"As iron sharpens iron, so one man sharpens another." (Proverbs 27:17)**.

To find out more about getting our basic needs met in Christ Jesus, we recommend doing the course 'I need someone to love me.'

Why Christians sometimes hurt one another

It is a sad fact that Christians do sometimes hurt one another. Why? There are many reasons and looking to people to meet our basic needs instead of to Jesus is just one of them.

Leaders who are insecure and feel threatened by something that is said or done to them may lash out defensively. Occasionally, we find a leader who is on some kind of power trip and instead of exercising their pastoral role with love, they seek to dominate and control. Such leaders put people down who should be lifted up and encouraged. When these issues are not addressed, they can cause havoc.

Action or reaction

When we get hurt, we have a choice. Are we going to act or react? Our natural instinct to react! Do you know that **no one can hurt us unless we let them**. Think about that! We can take the hurt on board or choose to throw it off onto Jesus and let Him show us what to do in the situation. Some might ask, "Why does God allow it to happen? I don't deserve this." God is into character building and He uses the trials of life to help us grow (see James 1:2-4) In a situation where we get hurt, misunderstood, rejected or passed over, we can bring it to God and ask "Father, what is it You want to teach me in all this?" If we expect Him to show us, He will. To vote with our feet and leave a church fellowship should only happen if the leader or other person involved has hardened their heart, is unwilling to discuss the problem and the peace of God departs. Whatever happens, our part is to forgive, seek God and, if we must move on, go where He leads. To stop going to church altogether because we are nursing our wounds will only lengthen the healing process. If it's right to move, finding a church fellowship where love is clearly evident among its members will hasten the healing process for us.

The joy of forgiveness

Some years ago my wife and I gave up our jobs and joined a ministry we felt God had led us to be part of and the leadership there felt it was right too. A few months later, a rapid promotion gave me access to confidential information and I discovered unrighteous dealings and understood why our salary had not been paid. What was I to do? I spoke to the leader who said the ministry had got off track and needed to be realigned. He arranged a series of meetings in which to seek the Lord. Instead of clarity, we had chaos because the Deceiver had been given a foothold. Jenny and I found ourselves being wrongly accused of bringing about this chaos. It was painful! People we had trusted with our livelihood and ministry had badly let us down.

But there was more to come! A few weeks later, the Trustees met and discovered unrighteous acts had penetrated other areas of the ministry. They informed us in the circumstances they had decided to close the whole work down. We were left homeless (with three young children), jobless and penniless. The temptation to give up on the Church was strong. The temptation to detest and have nothing more to do with those who had wrongly accused and let us down was doubly strong. But in our heart of hearts we knew that was wrong. After a bit of a struggle, we rolled the matter onto the Lord, choosing to forgive as He for Christ's sake forgave us. Before we left that part of the country, God, in answer to our prayers, gave us the opportunity to meet with our former leaders and tell them how we had felt, express our forgiveness and pray with them for their and our future. We felt released from that situation and our joy was restored. Though the months ahead were extremely difficult, we were able to look forward and not back.

No one listens

If we say that we feel no one listens to our point of view, is that really how it is or is it the case that we are peeved because we can't get our own way? If so, that is immature or – worse - wanting to dominate and control. It is normally good and right to express an opinion but if it doesn't reflect the prevailing view at the time we must rest in the fact that we have shared our views and leave it there. We may be right but the time is not right for such a view to be adopted. We need to let it go and allow God to bring it back. We need to allow Him time to change minds – yes, even ours, if that is what He wants to do.

Give it to Jesus

When we turn our hurts over to God and truly trust Him to deal with the matter, He will always show us what to do or change the situation. When we give it to Him and come to a place of peace, we can confidently expect some action. We might have to humble ourselves and submit. We might have to meet with the person concerned to try to sort things out. We might have to take the matter higher if there is another authority figure to turn to but we must, from the heart, forgive whoever has hurt us. If we have exhausted all possibilities for resolving the matter and found no desire on the part of those who caused the hurt to recognize what they have done, we might have to decide to find a new spiritual home. In this case, we must tell the leader why we are leaving, making sure there is no hostility on our part and tell the leader of the congregation we are led to join, exactly why we left our previous fellowship. Most important, we must then avoid speaking ill of the congregation/leader we have left.

Where were they when I needed them?
Was the Church aware of your need? Did you ask for help? When you do this, as well as encouraging you to look to God to meet your need, a leader will ask God if there is something he/she should do as part of God's answer to your prayer. The right way of helping may be to refer you to someone better equipped to deal with the matter. Crazy as it seems, some folk say to themselves "These people should know what I need so why aren't they helping me?" Sometimes people can discern a need but most often, they have to be told in order to be able to help. Our pride can keep us from making our needs known. We can be our own worst enemies. Whenever you have a need, swallow your pride and seek help. That way you will not be robbed of the assistance you need and the congregation may be blessed by being asked to help.

Get involved

Abandoning church altogether because they weren't there when you needed them only isolates you further. Talk to the leader about what you felt went wrong. If the leader was at fault in some way, he/she will want to do whatever they can to ensure no one else suffers in this way. Forgive and plunge right in again – get involved – enjoy the benefits of fellowship. God does care and wants you to be in a place to receive His grace, know His loving arms around you and be able to hear His voice.

The course 'Dealing with offence' gives valuable teaching on the 'if', 'how' and 'when' we should handle offence.

(Group H. Incorporating reasons 28 – 29)

Disappointed With God

If you say "I am disappointed with God," what are you really saying? That God has not come up to your expectation - not done what you asked Him to do? Consider carefully - is it His nature to have picked you out as one person to whom His promises do not apply? There is no evidence to show He has ever treated anyone who seeks Him with their whole heart in a way other than that which the Bible makes clear i.e. God loves us and wants a living relationship with us in which we experience more and more of Him and His goodness towards us.

Many promises are conditional

If you are disappointed with God, the likely reason is that either you have some wrong ideas about God or, for whatever reason you have not done your part to develop a relationship with Him where you know Him, His will for you and can truly trust Him.

Many people ask God for things as if He is a Father Christmas with a big sack just waiting to dole out whatever we want. Some make demands on God, thinking if they throw Scripture at Him this will move Him in their favour. God loves us and wants to answer our prayers but He has, for our own good, laid down some conditions and principles. In fact, many of the promises God has made in the Bible are conditional. He says "If you will, then I will". If we take time and effort to find out exactly what He says in His Word and the context in which He said it, we could save ourselves a lot of disappointment. Another fact is that answers to our prayers are sometimes delayed to test our faith and stimulate us to perseverance. At other times God may want to teach us something before granting our request.

If you have been disappointed with God, it just could be that you have never really got to know Him and His ways. The good news is that it is not too late to put this right. Begin to read about Him in the Bible, listen to good teaching tapes, get God TV and watch Him at work in these programmes, spend time with Him in prayer and get back to a church fellowship and get involved so as to grow spiritually. You will find God is faithful – He does what He says He will do if we play our part by wanting to please Him and do His will.

Is God really there?

If you say "I am not sure I believe in God anymore," who was the God you once believed in? Was it the God of the Bible who is love and who wants a relationship with us? Have you really sought Him and earnestly wanted to develop a right relationship with Him? Have you spent time in His Word and in prayer? He has promised **"...if...you seek the Lord your God, you will find Him if you look for Him with all your heart and with all your soul" (Deuteronomy 4:29)**. All who genuinely seek Him find Him. God is there waiting, with open arms to welcome you into fellowship with Him through Jesus.

(Group I. Incorporating reasons 30 – 31)

Unbelieving Partners

The apostle Paul was very aware of the difficulties of just one partner in a marriage being a Christian. It caused problems for some of the early believers; it can still cause difficulties and no doubt will do so until Jesus returns. This is why Paul advised the early Christians not to be "unequally yoked". This is a reference to two oxen pulling a plough. If they are not of more or less equal strength, the stronger one will be held back by the weaker one. Paul wasn't thinking about physical strength but spiritual strength. This was powerfully illustrated when, at a meeting for youth I attended, the speaker asked a young person representing the believer, to stand on a chair. Another person, of equal size and strength (representing the unbelieving partner) was then asked to stand beside the chair, hold hands with the person on the chair and both pull. The one on the chair was unable to pull the other person up to join them but the one on the ground found it easy to pull the other one off the chair.

Many a young Christian has got into a relationship with an unbeliever and lived to regret it. The full text of Paul's reference is this **"Do not be yoked together with unbelievers. For what do righteousness and wickedness have in common? Or what fellowship can light have with darkness? What harmony is there between Christ and Belial? What does a believer have in common with an unbeliever?" (2 Corinthians 6:14-15)**.

In congregations where there are few young people, it is not unusual for a young woman, planning on marrying an unbeliever to say, "But there were no suitable young men in my congregation." I wonder in these situations how much prayer ascends to heaven from the congregation on behalf of those seeking a marriage partner. Too often young people are left to get on with it. Church - we have a responsibility to support our young people in this way and encourage them to mix with young people from other congregations. Too often the fear of losing them to another congregation holds us back. God forgive us!

The believer with an unsaved partner usually just wants them to become as they are – a fully committed Christian. Paul assures us that unbelieving partners are 'sanctified' through the faith of the believing partner. What does this mean? The New Living Bible paraphrases the text concerned from 1 Corinthians 7:14 **"For the Christian wife brings holiness to her marriage, and the Christian husband brings holiness to his marriage."** What does it mean to bring holiness to the marriage? A holy person is one who is set apart from the world for the kingdom of God and led by the Holy Spirit. Therefore, their influence on the marriage should bring all the benefits of being led by the Spirit including the fruit of the Spirit, love, joy, peace, patience, kindness, goodness, faithfulness, gentleness and self control. Such influence is powerful – much more powerful for example than nagging one's partner to go to church.

Maintain a Spirit filled life

To maintain a Spirit filled life, the believing partner should take the opportunities for fellowship with other believers that church life offers and they must be firm about making time to develop their relationship with the Lord through reading the Bible and prayer at home. This, of course, doesn't mean deliberately choosing a time you know will cause problems. It is better to tell your partner your faith is important and helps you to do your part in keeping the marriage healthy. Explain that you need a daily quiet time with God and to regularly meet with other believers in the fellowship of the church. Then discuss how this can be arranged. Let him/her see by your lifestyle the difference time spent with the Lord and at church makes.

A young woman we know with an unsaved husband is so open about her faith, it is not unusual for him to ask her to find out God's view when a problem arises or a big decision has to be made. As a result, he wants to know more about her faith.

Making a stand

When the believer is expected to do all the giving and none of the taking, it's time to make a stand. Much wisdom and grace is needed in doing this – it can be costly. Ask God for His help in handling the matter and get the leaders of the church praying too. Come to a place of agreement in prayer with your leaders. God is faithful. He will guide you. Generally speaking, an unsaved partner will be more impressed by their believing partner's firm but gentle approach than by aggressive confrontation.

There will be times when being without your partner in a congregation where most others are married couples will make you feel out of it. However, it is a sad fact that many congregations have people whose partners come only occasionally or not at all. Press on in the knowledge that God understands and is with you. Resist the temptation to leave and the devil will flee from you.

Small group support

Many Christians with unsaved partners find a small group can be very beneficial because of the sense of belonging and the support such groups foster. A definition of 'support' is to 'give practical or emotional help to.' In these groups everyone can give as well as receive. Explaining this benefit to an unsaved partner who can't understand what the attraction is, must not leave them feeling inferior. God will give you the right words to use if His help is sought.

(Group J. Incorporating reasons 32 – 33)

Marriage And The Church

When marriage breaks down

The breaking of a vow is a very serious matter. In a Christian marriage it is particularly tragic because Christians know marriage is not man's idea but God's. Almost always, other people are also affected by a marriage breakdown - often for years afterwards. The Church expects marriage to last for life according to the vows taken and when it does not, the Church has to respond appropriately. How can it show compassion whilst maintaining that marriage vows should not be broken? On the surface it is clear cut. God hates divorce – the Bible says so - and those who get divorced are considered to be outside His will (except in special circumstances). On the other hand, God is gracious and compassionate and we know that a marriage breakdown is not the unpardonable sin!

If you have stayed away from church because of divorce, you may have done so unnecessarily. To find out more, we recommend the course 'After Divorce' which can be downloaded from the back2church website. (See 'Introduction to courses'). Don't let our enemy, Satan, keep you from getting an understanding of God's heart in the matter. God cares for you more than you may think!

Remarriage and the church

There is much misunderstanding of what the Bible has to say about divorcees and remarriage. As a result, some branches of the Church will not marry divorcees but others will under certain circumstances. If you have been through divorce and have remarried, or are contemplating re-marrying but have stopped going to church because you think they will be against it, you will find the course 'After Divorce' helpful. By doing the course you will gain an understanding of the issues involved and hopefully a way forward. God loves you whether or not you are a divorcee and He hasn't written you off. The course will help you to see something of the heart of God in this area.

Abortion

The Church in general has compromised its stand on the issue of abortion and as a result, confusion reigns! Feelings of guilt after abortion are common. However, it is not the unforgivable sin. Our course 'After abortion' gives helpful teaching on this matter. When God's view, as set out in the Bible is embraced, there is a way forward as our course shows.

(Group K. Incorporating reasons 34)

Getting Back To Church

Finding a church

A key question is what are you looking for in a church fellowship? The example we have of church in the New Testament is, as we have said, one where, in addition to evangelism, the following things are in place.

Worship, prayer, drawing close to God, the preaching of the Word, use of spiritual gifts, fellowship and encouragement.

A church fellowship without these things is without balance. However, important these things are, over-riding all them is love. **"All men will know that you are my disciples if you love one another." (John 13:35)**. Look for love and for some evidence of spiritual life. How will you recognise it? You will see it in the way you are welcomed into the building, by the way people relate to one another and try to include you, by their love and respect for the leaders and by the way the congregation is helped through preaching and prayer ministry to live out their faith in their everyday world. These things flow out of a heart of love for God. Most Christians will easily overcome frustrations with styles of worship, differences of direction and personal preferences if they know they are loved. It is conceivable that one may have to look beyond the immediate locality for such a fellowship but it will be worth it.

(Group L. Incorporating reason 35)

Getting To Church

Transport problems

Judging by most church car parks, those who walk to a church building these days are a minority. There are exceptions to this, of course, but people without transport may indeed have difficulty getting to a fellowship because public transport on a Sunday is a very much reduced service. Contact the church secretary – always a useful person to know – or the leader and make your needs known. Some churches collect people in a minibus, others have organised or informal systems for giving lifts. If someone gives you a lift, please show your appreciation. It costs nothing to say 'thank you' and you can find simple, inexpensive ways to show your gratitude now and then.

Getting To Church

uth, righteousness, peace, faith, salvatio
the Holy Spirit and the word of God

uth, righteousness, peace, faith, salvatio
the Holy Spirit and the word of God
uth, righteousness, peace, faith, salvatio
the Holy Spirit and the word of God
uth, righteousness, peace, faith, salvatio
the Holy Spirit and the word of God
uth, righteousness, peace, faith, salvatio
the Holy Spirit and the word of God
uth, righteousness, peace, faith, salvatio
the Holy Spirit and the word of God
uth, righteousness, peace, faith, salvatio
the Holy Spirit and the word of God
uth, righteousness, peace, faith, salvatio
the Holy Spirit and the word of God
uth, righteousness, peace, faith, salvatio
the Holy Spirit and the word of God
uth, righteousness, peace, faith, salvatio
the Holy Spirit and the word of God
uth, righteousness, peace, faith, salvatio
the Holy Spirit and the word of God

The Unspoken Reason

The most common, underlying reason people leave the fellowship of the church is not mentioned on our list because it is not one people are usually willing to give. It is this - when the enemy comes to undermine and bring to an end relationships in the Church with his lies, his seeds of doubt, his reasoned arguments, his cloak of self righteousness, his shackles of guilt or his tunic of pride, he often finds there is no armour of God to stop him. No belt of truth because the voice of the Spirit who guides into all truth has been silenced. There is no breastplate of righteousness – just one's own righteousness. The feet are not shod with the readiness that comes from the gospel of peace – this gospel has not yet been fitted. There is no shield of faith – only belief in what the eyes can see and in the rational. He finds no helmet of salvation in place to protect the mind and because the sword of the Spirit, the word of God is gathering dust on the bookshelf, there is no resistance. There is no praying in the Spirit - no call made on heaven for assistance.

In this spiritual battle the soldier of Christ was unprepared – he/she had nothing but the flesh with which to resist the enemy. As the hymn says, 'The arm of flesh will fail you.' And it did!

Is this all our fault? If we knew of these things and did nothing about them, yes, the responsibility is ours. If we were never taught these things, the church must shoulder a large share of the blame. I say 'share' because there is nothing that will stop those who really want to know the truth.

The good news is that God is not looking to blame anyone. His heart is to forgive – to see reconciliation take place – to welcome you home. He wants to cover the circumstances surrounding the decision to leave church with His grace. As we have said, He does not want the past to rob us of a glorious future.

It really is time to make a fresh start for all the reasons we give in the sections that follow.

"Finally, be strong in the Lord and his mighty power. Put on the full armour of God so that you can take your stand against the devil's schemes. For our struggle is not flesh and blood, but against the rulers, against the authorities, against the powers of this dark world and against the spiritual forces of evil in the heavenly realms. Therefore put on the full armour of God, so that when the day of evil comes, you may be able to stand your ground, and after you have done everything, to stand. Stand firm then, with the belt of truth buckled round your waist, with the breastplate of righteousness in place, and your feet fitted with the readiness that comes from the gospel of peace. In addition to all this, take up the shield of faith, with which you can extinguish all the flaming arrows of the evil one. Take the helmet of salvation and the sword of the Spirit, which is the word of God. And pray in the Spirit on all occasions with all kinds of prayers and requests. With this in mind, be alert and always keep on praying for all the saints."

(Ephesians 6: 10-18)

The Meaning Of 'Church'

What is church?

Ask a dozen people, "What is church?" and most will point to a building with a spire or tower or perhaps a simple hall with a label such as 'Baptist Church.' But these are just meeting places. Some will say the church is 'Christians' and in a sense, this is right because the **Church is the spiritual body of those who believe in the Lord Jesus Christ and are in relationship with Him.** (Regrettably, not everyone who calls themselves a Christian is in relationship with Christ or seeks to obey Him and as a result, true Christianity gets maligned).

When believers regularly meet for worship in any building they are collectively called 'the church congregation' and their involvement with one another we call 'the church fellowship.'

You are the church!

If you believe:

- Jesus is the Christ – the Anointed One – the Son of God
- That He was sent by the Father to take on our humanity, being born of the virgin Mary
- That He was crucified to take on Himself the punishment our sin deserves
- That He died, was buried but rose from the dead, appeared to many and then ascended to the Father victorious over our enemy Satan

If you have believed in Him and His redeeming work, have confessed, renounced and repented of your sin, asked for and received His forgiveness and invited Him to come and reign in your life by the indwelling of the Holy Spirit, **you are a part of the church which is His body**.

James Thwaites in his book 'The Church Beyond the Congregation' points to the big picture. "We are all called into the body of Christ – to see His church built in our marriages, our businesses, our homes, our work, our gathering together, our entire lives. We must release the powerful name 'church' to define all of life, work and relationships." Wherever you are – at home, school, work, leisure, or with other believers worshipping Him on Sunday, you are the church. This is awesome! But like ambassadors sent to represent their country, if we are to faithfully represent our King, we must maintain close contact with Him.

What did you think was the purpose of church services?

If we have wrong expectations of what the church is, we shouldn't be surprised if we find ourselves sitting in a congregation saying to ourselves, "What on earth am I doing here?" We need to know what the church is about otherwise it is easy to become critical of what goes on and get nothing out of the services. Since the Bible is the basis of the Christian faith we should also look there for the answer to the question, 'What is the purpose of the church?' Once we know the answer, it is easy for us to decide if we want to be part of it. It is worth spending a few minutes exploring this.

The origin of the church

The Christian church came into existence around 2000 years ago, after Jesus was crucified, rose from the dead to secure eternal life for those who believe He is who He said He is and choose to love Him and follow His ways. Jesus ascended to the Father and sent the Holy Spirit to be the comforter, guide and helper of those who believe in Him as well as giving them power to tell others the good news. The spiritual body of believers everywhere is called the Church. As we have said, if you have given your life to Jesus, you are part of the Church.

The purpose of church

Paul tells us in Ephesians 1:22-23 that the church is Christ's body. He describes it as **"the fullness of Him who fills all in all."** The purpose of the church is to be this fullness, to represent Jesus on earth and enforce the victory He won over the powers of darkness. The New Testament, as well as containing the true story of the life, death, burial, resurrection and ascension of Jesus and the coming of the Holy Spirit, also tells us of the birth of the church. Some of the church's growing pains and suffering are recorded there in Acts for our benefit. Practical details of how to live as part of the church are given in letters written by early leaders. To be the fullness of Christ Jesus i.e. to be like Him, we must study these things so as to get to know Him and His ways. The Church is responsible for helping us to become His well informed, well trained disciples who enjoy fellowship with Him.

A living relationship

Having a living relationship with God is never dull. In the Bible we see that those who surrendered their lives to Jesus Christ, found Him to be faithful when He said, **"I have come that they may have**

life, and have it to the full." (John 10:10). This fullness of life comes out of:

- A loving relationship with Jesus as Lord and Saviour
- The Holy Spirit's indwelling that brings understanding
- The power to live by the Spirit
- Holy Spirit-inspired boldness to tell others about Jesus
- Obedience to the prompting of the Holy Spirit to use His gifts, often with astonishing results
- Unspeakable joy
- Peace that passes understanding
- A love for Him and one another that keeps growing
- A vibrant coming together with other believers. Acts 2:42-43 describes it: **"They devoted themselves to the apostles' teaching and to the fellowship, to the breaking of bread and to prayer. Everyone was filled with awe, and many wonders and miraculous signs were done by the apostles."**

The more we spend time in getting to know our heavenly Father, the more we will appreciate what a truly wonderful God He is and just how very much He loves us. Then we will want to praise, worship and adore Him wherever we are and delight in doing so in the company of others who feel the same.

We see from Paul's letter to the church at Corinth that their coming together was sometimes chaotic. He said, **"Follow the way of love and eagerly desire spiritual gifts...When you come together, everyone has a hymn, or a word of instruction, a revelation, a tongue or an interpretation. All these must be done for the strengthening of the church. But everything must be done in a**

fitting and orderly way. For God is not a God of disorder but of peace." (1 Corinthians 14: 1, 26, 40, 33).

From history we see that much of this freedom in worship departed from the Church when a Roman Emperor allegedly became a Christian, made it the State religion and mixed pagan customs and costumes with the core values of the Church. Today God is bringing about a restoration of the values that matter to the church. Church is meant to be a joyful expression of believers' relationships with their loving heavenly Father and one another and the world. Just as ambassadors represent their country to another country, the Church as ambassadors of the Kingdom of God, must represent His fullness to the world and tell of the good news that the Kingdom of God has come and is coming demonstrating this as we experience in increasing measure the **"fullness of Him who fills everything in every way" (Ephesians 1:23)**. God is calling His church back to the New Testament model – sometimes whacky but wonderful and undergirded by love. Many church fellowships have responded to this call and the likelihood is there is one not too far from you.

The right reason

In summary then, there is only one right reason for being part of a congregation and that is a desire to develop one's relationship with Jesus Christ and His people so as to be equipped to be His ambassadors in the world. If you had some other motive, you should not be surprised it didn't work. However, belonging to a church fellowship for the right reason changes everything.

Attending church services is not enough

You may attend church services three times each Sunday, several times in the week, take responsibility for a part of the programme etc. and still miss out on the most important thing – your relationship with God. The relationship can be developed and expressed in serving others through the Church but unless time is spent in getting to know Him in our daily lives, it will not bear fruit. The key to knowing Him is to ask the Holy Spirit to fill you as you develop your spiritual life through prayer and spend time reading and studying the Bible.

"My son, do not forget my teaching,
but keep my commandments in your heart,
for they will prolong your life many years
and bring you prosperity.
Let love and faithfulness never leave you.
Trust in the Lord with all your heart
and lean not on your own understanding
in all your ways acknowledge him
and he will make your path straight."
(Proverbs 3:1-3,5&6)

In Hosea 4:6 it is written that the Lord said, **"My people are destroyed from a lack of knowledge."** This is true of many believers today. Because they don't know the Bible and because they have not fed their spirit and soul on its nourishing food, they fall when temptation or trials come. Often church leaders are at fault for not teaching the value and relevance of the Bible to our everyday lives when it is one of a Christian's most powerful weapons against the attacks of the enemy. Make no mistake, such leaders will be judged severely for this. God cares for us so much, He gave us His Word for every occasion. Making a priority of studying the Word under the guidance of the Holy Spirit and anointed teachers will enable us to act in a right manner in all circumstances. It saves us from the lies of Satan who would love us to focus on the problem instead of the Word of God.

"Men ought always to pray.
When you pray, go into your room,
close the door and pray to your Father.
Watch and pray so that you will not
fall into temptation.
Whatever you ask for in prayer,
believe that you have received it,
and it will be yours.
Pray without ceasing."
(Luke 18:1, Matthew 6:6, 26:41,
21:22, 1 Thessalonians 5:17)

There is no doubt, prayer gets better the more we get into it. When we discover prayer changes things – though we may need to persist, we realize what a wonderful blessing it is that we can really talk to God and He hears us. There are some excellent books on prayer available through Christian bookshops and church bookstalls. Some suggestions for reading are made in the section 'Resources.'

Why Get Back Into The Fellowship Of The Church?

Here are seven good reasons for getting back into the fellowship of the church.

1. God loves you

The Bible is clear - God loves us and wants us to enjoy a loving relationship with Him; it is a fundamental part of the Christian gospel.

Being told God loves you is one thing, knowing He loves you is another. Isn't it like that in our human relationships? She may say she loves him (and that's good to hear) but to be convinced, he needs to know it is true. How does she show it is true? By her actions – tenderness towards him, wanting to please him, doing things together, talking, sharing and giving presents. By gently pulling him up when he is wrong and accepting correction when she is. By building him up when he is down and being built up by him. She will have eyes only for him, reassuring him she will not stray. All these things require constant communication. This is a picture of God's love for us. God has told us He loves us in His word, the Bible: **"I have loved you with an everlasting love; I have drawn you with loving-kindness." (Jeremiah 31:3)**. He has also shown us by His actions that He loves us – it is not just words, although they are very important. God does both! When God created mankind He was pleased with what He had made but we turned our backs on Him and believed the lies of Satan* instead. The Bible tells us that **"all have sinned and fall short of the glory of God..." (Romans 3:23)** and the inevitable result of turning our backs on God our Creator is a sense of separation from Him. But still God loved us and found a way to satisfy His perfect justice, enabling us to be forgiven. We deserved to die but He sent His Son to die instead – to take the punishment we deserve. Jesus, God's only Son was put to death on a cross though He had done no wrong, and God laid on Him the sins of the world. In John 3:16 it says: **"God so loved the world that He gave His one and only Son, that whoever believes in Him shall not perish but have eternal life."** That is fantastic news! We can be forgiven and begin a new and loving relationship with God through His Spirit living within us if we will:

- Confess our sin – admit we are wrong
- Renounce – give up our sinful ways
- Repent – change our minds and turn around from doing things our way toward His way
- Believe Jesus is who He said He is, that He died - thereby paying the ransom for us - and that He rose from the dead
- Ask for and receive the forgiveness that results from this sacrifice
- Make Him (who ascended to the Father and now intercedes for us), the Lord of our lives
- Invite His Spirit to live in us
- Make getting to know Him and His ways a priority through reading the Bible, talking with Him in prayer, having fellowship with other believers and availing ourselves of the teaching and ministry of the Church.

This new relationship with God is just for starters – He has done so much more for us than can be said now. The way we find out more is through the reading and study of His Word, the Bible, by letting His Holy Spirit teach us, by talking to Him in prayer and putting ourselves under the teaching and instruction of anointed church leaders. It is in the fellowship of the Church that we discover how to apply what we learn. There we will find people who, having discovered these things themselves and as a result are full of the joy of the Lord, love to talk to others about what they have learned. There we sharpen each other up in our faith as **"iron sharpens iron." (Proverbs 27:17)**. There we encourage one another, pray for one another and hear God together. Isn't this enough reason for wanting to get back into the fellowship of the church now?

The course 'I need someone to love me' has more to say about His wonderful love for us.

Yes, there really is an adversary doing his best to undermine all that is good. Satan is a fallen angel cast out of heaven, who Jesus described as* *"a murderer from the beginning, not holding to the truth, for there is no truth in him. When he lies, he speaks his native language, for he is a liar and the father of lies." (John 8:44)****. However, the good news is,* ***"The reason the Son of God appeared was to destroy the devil's work."***

(1 John 3:8)*.*

2. The God-sized slot

We have already said God created us to have a loving relationship with Him. His very nature is love. Our ability to respond to His love was built into us when we were created. We sometimes call it the 'God-sized slot'. Until it is filled, we will always have a sense of something missing. People from all walks of life have experienced this emptiness and may spend a great deal of time, money and energy trying to find something that will fill the void. They try money, sex, power, false religions, drugs, alcohol, one therapy after another, different relationships and so on. Though good, the best of our human relationships will not satisfy our inner need.

It is because men and women have turned their back on God that this need is not met. God, who we have already said loves us with an everlasting love, has the answer. It is Jesus! If we turn around in repentance from trying to manage without Him and move towards Him, we will see not an angry God but one who wants to forgive. No one who sincerely asks for forgiveness will be denied. **"Whoever comes to Me I will never drive away...everyone who looks to the Son and believes in Him shall have eternal life, and I will raise him up at the last day." (John 6:37&40)**. Having asked for and received forgiveness, God then places His Holy Spirit within us. He satisfies us - He is both the water and the bread of life.

We may discover these things reading the Bible and good Christian books, listening to tapes, watching Christian teaching videos etc. but it is in church, the fellowship of believers, that we not only learn these truths but also have the opportunity to work out this knowledge in our lives with the support of other believers. Then, because the experience is so satisfying, we will want to tell others the good news. This is the way the Kingdom of God grows.

3. The church is the body of believers

We, the Church, may have made a mess of it but the Bible clearly teaches that we are His messenger to the world. God has no Plan B! The Church has much to repent of and all over the country there are congregations who are recognising this. As they seek His pardon, commit themselves to His purposes as outlined in His word and allow the Holy Spirit to take the lead, new life is coming to these fellowships.

In many countries throughout the world, Christians are being persecuted for their faith. In some places, church buildings are being burned down and believers are forbidden to meet. Why? Enemies of the Church know that without opportunity to meet, believers become isolated from the support of their congregation and some crack denying their faith.

Church fellowships who have failed to show the love of God, have watered down God's Word or refused to allow the Holy Spirit to lead them, may continue for a while although people are deserting such fellowships in great numbers. It is not surprising many church buildings have closed. If you have been disappointed with a church fellowship, the answer is not to stay away but to find one that is moving on with God. The devil is well pleased when we opt out instead of finding a better option. Further help is available in the section 'Getting back or moving on' and the course 'Dealing with offences'.

4. God is waking His church

It's about a hundred years since the great Welsh Revival, when God's Holy Spirit came with such power on ordinary people that thousands were convicted of the sin in their lives and found mercy. Their lives were transformed with the healing of sickness and infirmities, deliverance from strongholds of the devil and other great changes for the good. The atmosphere in many towns and villages, shops, offices, factories and mines changed from one of oppressive darkness to one of light and joy. Sadly, the revival only lasted a few years but many believe God was demonstrating how it will be when, as promised, He pours out his Spirit in these last days. God is waking His church. Where church fellowships are open to Him, earnestly seek Him in prayer and live according to His Word and the flow of His Spirit, people are turning to Jesus for Salvation, and healing is taking place. Those bound by the devil are being set free and the love of God is most wonderfully present. We hear much about the shrinking number of people who attend traditional church buildings but little about those that are being wakened and the new fellowships being established - replacing those that are dead. In a letter to the Daily Mail 28-1-04, the Rev. J Willan of Church Survey UK said, "Churches don't grow by having gimmicks but by providing four basic things:

i. Clear teaching on moral topics

ii. Clergy who actively visit their community

iii. Clear explanations as to why believing in the Bible makes sense, with evidence from archaeology and fulfilled Bible prophecy

iv. Clear presentation of God's character as being Holy and not just some kind of 'Father Christmas' figure in the sky

I would add a fifth

v. Believers whose lives reflect the presence of Jesus wherever they go

If the church fellowship you left doesn't match up to this new thing God is doing, don't go there. Search for one that is. However, you must be willing to let God change you. Put the past behind you. Let it go – move on with God. Doing some of the courses on our website may help you in this.

5. A morally bankrupt society

A Christian pastor and teacher who spent years studying these things said recently that between them, the European Economic Community and the Government of Great Britain have passed laws in the last 10 years that have broken every one of the Ten Commandments! Bear in mind these Ten Commandments have been the basis of our legal systems (and that of many other countries) for hundreds of years. This is a very serious matter. Without God, we put in place legislation to create a humanistic society that permits the things God in His wisdom told us not to do for our own good. Humanism is the belief that man is the central reference point of life and meaning, thus exalting human wisdom above the revelation of God.

We are already reaping the harvest of pain, suffering and broken relationships resulting from a liberal approach to marriage, sex and abortion. There is more to come as other Christian values we once held dear are eroded and replaced with increasing permissiveness. Man without God is corrupt, as is so visible in countries that have tried to shut Him out altogether. Will we never learn?

The Church has been weakened in its ability to stand against humanism and the liberal approach to morality, by division, denominational differences and a refusal to give the Holy Spirit freedom to carry out His agenda. These things have caused many to forsake the Church and so it has become numerically weak. Where it should be shouting these things from the roof top and demanding change for the good, the Church's voice is hardly heard in the corridors of power. This decline must be stopped for the sake of our nation and our children. A strong Church will be required to do this. The good news is that there are church fellowships, traditional and new, that are growing and taking on the forces of darkness, believing if we repent and cry out to Him, He will break out again as He did in Wales a century ago - but this time the effects will remain. We want to be part of that, don't you?

6. There is joy in Jesus

We have already mentioned the fact that when we make Jesus Lord, the emptiness we once experienced is no more. We are satisfied by His presence in our lives. We no longer have to search for something to fill the void. Our God-sized slot is full and running over. Glory to God! What a wonderful Saviour! What a great place to be in! But what is it we are being filled with? Jesus tells us in John's gospel. **"If you obey my commandments, you will remain in my love, just as I have obeyed my Father's commandments and remain in his love. I have told you this so that my joy may be in you and that your joy may be complete. My commandment is this: Love each other as I have loved you." (John 15:10-12)**. The Spirit of Jesus – the Holy Spirit - is a spirit of love, joy, peace, patience, kindness, goodness, faithfulness, gentleness and self control. So many good things – no wonder we call the gospel Good News.

When we surrender our lives fully to Him and live by the Holy Spirit, we discover this joy really exists and that God has a plan for our lives and all the resources needed to put it into effect. Those who have discovered this have had a huge impact on world history and found immense satisfaction as they have gone about it. Yes, there may be tears because the troubles God allows to test and make us strong can be tough at the time, but once the lesson has been learned, as Paul says, all things do work together for our good. There is nothing as good as knowing one is forgiven, doing the will of God and can expect to spend eternity with Him. Is it any wonder we can't contain ourselves and want the joy of sharing this good news with others?

7. It's later than you think!

All over the world, respected men and women of God from a variety of church streams are saying the same thing. These are the last days! Prophecies of the Old and New Testaments concerning the end of the age are being fulfilled – both the good and the bad. Jesus told His disciples to be ready because the Son of Man will come at an hour when people do not expect Him.

Believers should not be taken by surprise however, because the Bible tells them to watch for the signs of Jesus' impending return in nature, people's behaviour and extraordinary happenings, so they are ready.

Science can account for many of the unusual things happening in nature today but the increase in these events has been unpredictable – famines, plagues, floods, earthquakes etc.

Where people's behaviour is concerned, who would have imagined atrocities such as the Holocaust. Since then, political expediency and despotic leaders have combined to eliminate millions of innocent people. It is currently estimated there are 6 million Christians suffering various forms of persecution around the world. Lawlessness is on the increase, more children than ever are turning against their parents. Drug and alcohol abuse is multiplying, sexual diseases are at epidemic proportions and new diseases resistant to scientific remedies are appearing. In the financial realm billions are repeatedly wiped off the stock markets and fraud of previously unimaginable proportions is discovered with increasing frequency. Another oil crisis and who knows what will happen? Another crash of confidence in economic growth and more tragedy will follow.

Now we hear that a 'chip' has been developed the size of a grain of rice that is being inserted in the hand or forehead of some wealthy people as a means by which they can be tracked by satellite in the event of abduction. At least one country is considering this as a national identity system that its citizens must accept. So close have we come to the reality of Revelations 13:16.

One wonders how much more of man's arrogance God will tolerate. How much further down the genetic engineering road will we go before He says for our own good, "Enough is enough!"

In His Word, God tells us His Spirit will not always strive with man (Genesis 6:3). There is a "make-up-your-mind" time for all of us with eternal consequences.

On the positive side, Bible prophecies about an end-time harvest for the Kingdom of God are also being fulfilled. Revival is breaking out all over the world – often in places where the Church is suffering the harshest persecution. Millions are turning to Jesus Christ for forgiveness and a new beginning. The dark cloud of unbelief, of humanism and false religion across Europe will be dispersed as the Church increasingly unites in prayer and its leaders reach out in love for one another. It is beginning to happen! Glory to God! Our enemy Satan can see what is happening and is preparing to strike back. When persecution comes to us – there are already signs it is on its way – we will need one another more than ever.

Whether Christ comes back in our lifetime, (as many think is a real possibility the rapid way in which things are moving), or we die first, the best way is to be prepared – to enjoy God's presence now and be fulfilled by doing His good will for us. Being part of His Body on earth, the Church is where He wants to find us whenever our time is up.

Back to church - now

Of all the reasons for a return to the fellowship of the Church now, the most important is that God has chosen the Church as the conveyor of the good news that all can get to enjoy Him in His fullness, that our enemy has been overcome and we can spend eternity with Him. The world needs this good news but the making of disciples, those who are willing to make knowing Him and serving Him their number one priority, requires the ministry as well as the mission of the Church. **"His intent was that now, through the Church, the manifold wisdom of God should be made known to the rulers and authorities in the heavenly realms, according to his**

eternal purpose which He accomplished in Christ Jesus our Lord." (Ephesians 3:10).

Just as the Word says **"When you are tempted, He will also provide a way out so that you can stand up under it." (1 Corinthians 10:13)**, so when we are tempted to leave the fellowship of a church, He provides a way - grace to deal with the problem or a new place to go. Our task is to seek and obey Him – now! It is not too late! Don't be fooled by that deception. Jesus, who said, **"I will build My church..." (Matthew 16:8)** is waiting with open arms to welcome you home to His Church.

Beware The Comfort Zone

When people stop being part of a church fellowship, they may find doing their own thing on a Sunday and other times makes a nice change. Soon they find the time that was given to church gets filled with other things. Time spent with the Lord in prayer and in His Word then comes under pressure as the enemy tries to squeeze out the last vestiges of active faith. It may just take months – it may take years but without the ministry of the Church, we are increasingly vulnerable.

Those who used to give a lot of time and energy to the fellowship, after the initial strangeness of having all this time to themselves, may very well begin to relax and enjoy it. They may experience some guilt but otherwise feel better for it. Some may even have regrets so much time was spent 'doing church' at the expense of other things – especially family.

On leaving a church fellowship, friendships begin to change. The company of former church friends may make you feel uncomfortable, however accepting they are. Subtly, new 'non church' friends begin to change the things we do and the way we think. Compromise becomes easier and before we know it, even though we said we would never let it happen, we become just like them.

No one said being an active member of a church fellowship would be easy. You knew that when you 'signed up' and if you put your whole heart into your relationship with God, you'll have found there is no other way to real joy and satisfaction. However serious the problem may have been, to walk away from church altogether is to walk into the arms of temptation – the deceptive comfort zone.

There is an alternative way - let the trials of church life work for you. Take hold of the words of James 1:2-4 & 12. **"Consider it pure joy, my brothers, whenever you face trials of many kinds, because you know that the testing of your faith develops perseverance. Perseverance must finish its work so that you may be mature and complete, not lacking anything.**
Blessed is the man who perseveres under trial, because when he has stood the test, he will receive the crown of life that God has promised to those who love Him."

It's time to get back to God, back to His ways, back to church.

Getting Back Or Moving On

Our earnest desire is that many who visit the back2church website and read this book will, as a result, seriously think about getting back into the church fellowship to which they belonged or, where that fellowship has not fulfilled its role, move on to another place of Christian worship where the love of God is evident.

Getting back

Going through the doors of the church building again can be daunting. If you are concerned about this and know someone who is part of the fellowship, arrange for them to walk in with and sit with you. If you don't know who to contact or are now living in a new area, you could call the leader and ask for someone to look out for you if you don't just want to just turn up. If you pray before setting out, asking God to help you - rest assured He will.

Hopefully you will find love and acceptance and be glad to be back.

Moving on

If going back to the fellowship you left is not practical or you want to make a fresh start, how does one find a suitable place of worship?

- Pray about it – ask God to guide you to where He wants you
- Look in the telephone directory under 'Places of worship'. If you visit the back2church website and look at 'Supporters List' you will see websites of fellowships you might also like to consider

- Consider the benefits of being part of the church in the local community and the ease with which you can take along others you are trying to introduce to Christianity
- Look for love! If you ask Him, God will help you discern if His love is permeating the congregation and leadership. If it isn't, you really need the peace of God to confirm you should stay there
- Look for the other signs of a congregation that is moving on with God, as mentioned under the section, 'The meaning of Church'.

When you get back into fellowship, do tell us about it. We would love to pray for you.

"Let us not give up meeting together, as some are in the habit of doing, but let us encourage one another – and all the more as you see the Day approaching." (Hebrews 10:25)

It's time...

Part 2

John Jarvis

Suggestions For Prayer

Here are some suggestions for prayer. Many who use them tell of the wonderful change that has taken place as a result. So be encouraged! There does seem to be real benefit in:
a) speaking the prayers out loud to our Father God
b) speaking them out in the presence of someone you trust or
c) telling someone as soon as possible afterwards, what you have prayed

We like to hear of answers to prayer – it's encouraging and if we are permitted to tell others of the answers you have received, it could help them too. To tell us by e-mail, send your message to admin@back2church.org or write to us at the address given under the section Resources.

A prayer for salvation and to become a Christian

Almighty God, thank You for loving me. I have heard the good news of what You have done for me in Jesus. I believe He is Your only begotten Son, who came to earth, laying aside His majesty to take on our humanity and was crucified for my sins. I believe He died, rose again and is now with You until He returns for His Church. I confess I have tried to manage without You and have broken Your laws. Today I give up that way of life and turn towards You and Your ways. Please forgive my sins, washing them away through the blood of Jesus. By faith I now receive Your forgiveness and thank You for accepting me as Your child who is loved by You. I also receive the promise of eternal life for which I thank You with all my heart. Please help me by Your Holy Spirit within me to get to know You, to love You and live to please You. I ask this in the Name of Jesus. Amen.

A prayer for baptism in the Holy Spirit

Father God, Jesus said You love to give good gifts to your children and that You will give the Holy Spirit to those who ask. Father, although I have the Holy Spirit in me, I need to be filled with His presence and power to live to please You and witness to what Jesus has done for me. Therefore I ask that The Holy Spirit will fill every part of my life. I ask too for the gifts of the Holy Spirit to enable me to be more effective in speaking about You and building up the Church. I want the fruit of the Holy Spirit in my life so that I can become a true ambassador of my Lord and Saviour.

Father, I realise the measure of my being filled will be my emptiness of self. I therefore bring to the cross and leave there all self-seeking, selfish ambition and pride and ask You, in the Name of Jesus, to fill me now to overflowing. I believe as I ask, I receive and thank You Father. Hallelujah! Glory to God!

Expect to receive a joy such as you have not had since the day you were saved and the ability to speak in a language you haven't learned and don't understand. This is the gift of tongues – a prayer language the use of which will build up your spirit as the Holy Spirit prays through you. Ask for and expect to receive other gifts too, especially that you will prophecy. To find out more about the gifts of the Holy Spirit and how they should be used, get a copy of 'True Spirit' by Colin Urquhart, available from Christian bookshops or from Kingdom Faith Resources.

A prayer of repentance

Father God, I thank You that when Jesus was crucified, He bore my guilt and shame. Thank You for such love which I don't deserve and can't earn. Thank You Jesus for choosing to die for me. Father, I need forgiveness for I have sinned against You and (name any persons or organisation that you have sinned against and the nature of the sins)...

Father, I choose to give up sinning in these ways. I have changed my mind so that from this moment on I am walking away from sin towards You and Your ways. I will seek the forgiveness of those I have wronged and make restitution as necessary. Please forgive me and wash me clean through the blood of Jesus now. (As you receive your forgiveness, which happens the moment you ask, go on to say) - Father, I gratefully receive forgiveness on the basis of Your Word that says, **"If we confess our sins, He is faithful and just and will forgive us our sins and purify us from all unrighteousness." (1 John 1:9)** Thank You I am now made clean. Glory to God! When temptation comes, please remind me to submit to You, to resist the devil and then he will flee from me. (James 4:7). I ask this in the Name of Jesus. Amen.

A prayer for physical healing

(Before making this prayer, be sure to have removed any of the hindrances to your prayer mentioned in the Healing and Reconciliation Course.)

Father God, I thank You for Jesus and all that He has done for me. According to Your Word, by His wounds we have been healed - 1Peter 2:24 and in Psalm 103:2-3, it tells me not to forget all His benefits saying, **"He forgives all my sins and heals all my diseases."** I am therefore to bless the Lord from my inmost being. Father, I bring the sickness/disease that is in my body to the cross of Jesus where it has already been dealt with, and claim my healing in the name of Jesus. I receive that healing now for which I bless Your holy Name (Continue to bless the Lord daily for your healing whether it manifests in your body immediately or later. EXPECT!)

A prayer for emotional healing

(This prayer should be prayed in the presence of someone you trust and who knows and believes God's Word. It will be helpful to have pen and paper handy as indicated below. Read the prayer through first so as to be prepared and then prayer it aloud).

Father God, I thank You that You know my inmost being. There is nothing about me or my life that is unknown to You. Psalm 139 tells **me, "You created my inmost being; You knit me together in my mother's womb. I praise You because I am fearfully and wonderfully made... How precious to me are Your thoughts, O God."** The hurtful things I have stored away, not wanting to face or not knowing how to handle, are no surprise to You and are not beyond Your healing power.

Father, I also know that for healing to take place, these hurts must be brought to the light of Your love, confessed and renounced. (1 John 1:9) Holy Spirit, I ask you now to bring to mind situations, people or events that I need to expose to the light. *(Pause to allow the Holy Spirit to bring these things to mind. Write them down so that you can name them in a little while)*. Then go on to say:

Father, Your Word tells me that the truth will set me free (John 8:32). I want to be free and so I ask for courage to acknowledge the truth about each situation You have brought to mind, however painful or distressing this might be. *(Now go to your notes and pray about each item one at a time in this way).*

Since forgiveness is a key to my freedom in Christ, I here and now choose to forgive *(name the first person or organization on your list)* for the hurt they caused *(name the hurt)*. I renounce all hatred and any evil I have wished on them. I renounce all revenge and instead ask You, Father, to deal with them. Father God, I ask Your forgiveness for my wrong attitude and past unwillingness to forgive. I thank You that your Word tells me that if I forgive others, I too will be forgiven through Jesus (Matthew 6:14). I claim and receive that forgiveness and healing now. I renounce that evil and its effect on my life and declare I am washed clean by the blood of Jesus. *(Repeat this in respect of each item on your list and then go on to say…).*

Help me to remember Your faithfulness whenever the enemy, Satan, tries to bring this matter up again. On the basis of Your Word – Psalm 103:7, **"as far as the east is from the west, so far have You removed my transgressions from me,"** and according to 1 John 1:9, **"I am made clean from all unrighteousness."** Please fill me anew with The Holy Spirit (expect!). I ask this in the name of Jesus. Amen.

A prayer to be reconciled

(For this prayer to be effective you must first: a) forgive those to whom you wish to be reconciled and b) have asked for and received God's forgiveness for your part.)

Father God, in this matter of a breakdown in my relationship with *(name the person or organization)* I acknowledge I must first be reconciled to You. Father, I therefore ask for Your forgiveness, choose let go of all resentment, bitterness and unkind things I have said or thought about this person/persons or organization. I change my mind and choose to do away with pride and instead forgive them. I want to be reconciled to them if they are willing. Give me wisdom to know how to go about putting things right. Help me to say the right words in expressing my forgiveness and/or apologies. As I do so, let Your love flow into the relationship and let reconciliation take place. Father, if my approach is rebuffed, help me to roll the situation on to You and trust You to work it out. Thank You for Your great love for me and what Jesus did for me on the cross in reconciling me to You. You are so good to me! In Jesus' name. Amen.

A prayer for guidance when making decisions

Thank You Father God, that You know and care about the decisions we have to make. I am thankful too that **"the entrance of Your words gives light..." (Psalm 119:130)** I choose therefore to bring the light of Your Word to bear on this situation. You never ask me to do something that contradicts Your Word, so please show me the principles that must guide my decision. Please speak to my heart as I study Your Word and confirm it with Your peace and the witness of someone I respect. In Jesus' name I ask this. Amen.

A prayer confirming a decision to be a giver

Father God, who freely gives us all things to enjoy and Who has made precious promises to those who cheerfully give from all that You have given to them, today I choose to be a giver. I want to give generously, not begrudging or stingily but out of a heart full of love and thankfulness for all You have done for me in Christ Jesus. I want to give in faith trusting You as the Lord, our Provider (Genesis 22:14) and the One who gives power to generate wealth (Deuteronomy 8:18). I submit my finances to You, wanting to learn, **"the secret of being content in any and every situation..." (Philippians 4:12)**. I will regularly bring my gift into the storehouse, the church, and will sow offerings over and above this when and where I am directed by the Holy Spirit. This I do cheerfully, thanking You for the privilege of this practical expression of my love. Keep me faithful in this matter. In Jesus' name I ask. Amen.

A prayer that I may know the love of God

Father God, You know how I long to be loved and accepted. Your Word tells me You are love and that love comes from You (1 John 4:7-8). I therefore want to know You and the love You have for me. Your Word also tells me that, **"This is how God showed his love among us: He sent His one and only Son into the world that we might live through Him. This is love: not that we loved God, but that He loved us and sent His Son as an atoning sacrifice for our sins." (1 John 4:9-10)** Thank You Jesus for such incredible love. Father God, please wash me clean through the blood of Jesus, come and live in me by Your Holy Spirit and give me the faith to believe that I am loved by You. Since Your Word says, **"He who asks, believing, receives." (Matthew 21:22)**, having asked, I now believe I have received Your love. Thank You that according to 1 John 4:15-16, You – the God of love - now live in me and I in You, so I know and now rely on the love You have for me. I want to learn more about Your love, to trust You and be obedient to You. Help me to really get to know You through

Your Word and the fellowship of the Church. I ask this in the name of Jesus. Amen.

A prayer for courage to make a stand

(when family or friends ridicule or otherwise oppose my faith and/or my return to church)

Father God, I know Jesus warned us opposition would come and that many of my brothers and sisters in Christ in different parts of the world suffer for their faith. Thank You for their courage and example. In my situation I want to be obedient and to bless those who oppose me. Help me to show them love by not retaliating or withholding friendship. Please open my eyes to see opportunities to give to them a reason for my faith and help me do it in a way that is gracious but firm. I ask this in Jesus' name. Amen.

A prayer for courage to get back into the fellowship of the church

Father God, thank You for speaking to my heart about this matter. I know I should get back into the fellowship of the Church and not put it off. Father, it's been some time and my mind is full of 'what if's' and 'what will they think or ask'. Such thoughts are from fear; not of faith and not of You. I therefore reject these thoughts and place my hand in Yours, trusting You to give me courage as You lead and help me over the threshold and to the right seat. I affirm I will answer any questions put to me truthfully and gracefully. During the service help me to focus on You and worship You with all of my heart. Help me allow You to speak to me through what is said and to enjoy the fellowship. I ask this in the name of Jesus. Amen.

Declaration To Be Spoken Aloud!

I now look forward to getting back into the fellowship of the church and to a new relationship with my heavenly Father and His people. I will, by the grace of God, get back to Church starting

____

(Make it as soon as possible).

It's time... to come home

It's time...

Introduction To Courses

John Jarvis

INTRODUCTION TO COURSES

Our aim is to make the following courses available for downloading free on the back2church website and in hard copy at a charge on request during 2005. Please watch the website News page for release dates. The courses will greatly assist those who want to look in more detail at the Christian faith, the purpose of church and our role in it. Some courses have a Course Workbook. Details of how to download from the website (or obtain hard copies) are given on the website. Readers without access to the web will find details of how to obtain printed copies under the section Resources.

We aim to encourage churches to run live courses because of the value and fun of doing things together. To check if there is a live course running at a church near you, go to the News page of the website. To make e-mail enquiries about live courses send to admin@back2church.org

Course No.1: I need someone to love me

The most wonderful news the Church has is that God is love. We all need to be loved but often look for it in the wrong places. The course looks at our efforts to find satisfying love and shows how this need can be fully met in Jesus, who so loved us He gave His life for us. Learn more about this amazing love and how you can delight in its warm embrace.

Course No.2: A fresh start

In this course the question 'Why?' is frequently asked. Why should I believe in God? Why believe what the Bible says? Why did Jesus die and rise again? And so much more. This is an opportunity to explore Christianity's basic beliefs and what these have to do with us.

Course No.3: Dealing with offences

How should we respond to those who hurt us? If we don't react, how will justice be done? What if the hurts are so deep we feel we can't forgive? These and many more questions are discussed along with a godly way of handling relationships, preventing them from going wrong and enabling the healing of past wounds.

Course No.4: Physical and emotional healing

Does Jesus still heal today? What did He tell the church about healing? Can I be healed? What if my problem is more emotional than physical? Is there hope for me? In this course, the good news about healing is explained and help given in overcoming the various hindrances we may meet.

Course No.5: After divorce

"I have been through divorce - does this mean I am excluded from the Church? Has Christianity written me off?" The course looks at biblical teaching on the subject of marriage, divorce and the church and shows God's love remains even if we get it wrong.

Course No.6: After abortion

The emotional turmoil that often follows abortion as well as the disapproval of some sections of society and of the Church can leave one feeling rejected by both. Is this what the Church is really saying? Is this what God is saying? The course looks at the issues from the point of view of the parent(s), family, society and the Church and points to a way through.

Course No.7: Standing firm – more than conquerors

Many Christians feel a failure. They read about those who are strong in the faith and may even know some, but they seem to fall down again and again. Some are so disheartened they have given up. This course, in the form of a 31-day devotional booklet, reminds readers of the basic truths, which if they stand by them, will help them to avoid pitfalls and grow to become **"more than conquerors"**.

Further courses will be added from time-to-time.

It's time...

Resources

John Jarvis

Resources

Recommended books

'True Spirit' Colin Urquhart Kingdom Faith Ministries

'Forever Ruined for the Ordinary' Joy Dawson Thomas Nelson publishers

'An Affair of the heart' Robert Warren Highland Books

'The Bondage Breaker' and others in the Freedom in Christ series
Dr. Neil Anderson Monarch Books

'End time Events' Charles Capps Harrison House

'Bringing Home the Prodigals' Rob Parsons Care for the Family

'The Purpose Driven Life' Rick Warren Zondervan

Other

The Bible – New International Version

The Bible – New American Standard Version

The Amplified Bible

'The Word for Today' Daily Reading e-mail ucb@ucb.co.uk

'Pursuit of His presence' – Daily devotions
- Kenneth & Gloria Copeland Harrison House

Useful websites

www.uk.alphacourse.org
www.prodigals.org.uk
www.findachurch.co.uk

Readers who are unable to order obtain hard copies of this book using the Internet can order by phone or write for further information to:-

Back2church Resources
Kingsland Church, Lexden
2 London Road
Colchester CO3 4DE

Phone 01206 517580
e-mail admin@back2church.org

Notes

Notes

Notes